N⁰. X.

SELECTED BUSINESS DOCUMENTS

OF THE

NEO-BABYLONIAN PERIOD

BY

ARTHUR UNGNAD, PH. D.

OF THE ROYAL MUSEUM AT BERLIN

WIPF & STOCK • Eugene, Oregon

Wipf and Stock Publishers
199 W 8th Ave, Suite 3
Eugene, OR 97401

Selected Business Documents of the Neo-Babylonian Period
By Ungnad, Arthur
ISBN 13: 978-1-60608-352-9
Publication date 12/02/2008
Previously published by Brill, 1908

TO MY ESTEEMED TEACHER

PROFESSOR DR. FRIEDRICH DELITZSCH

AS A SMALL TOKEN OF GRATITUDE

INTRODUCTION

The neo-babylonian Business Documents or so-called contract-literature extends over a period from the time of Sennacherib down to the latest period of cuneiform-writing [1]). The great political revolutions of that whole epoch, especially the termination of Assyrian rule over Babylon [2]) and the capture of that city by Cyrus (539 B. C.) did not exert any noteworthy influence upon this kind of Babylonian literature. I have restricted myself in the present volume to business documents written before the Persian domination [3]), since the editors of the Study Series have reserved a separate volume for documents of the Persian period.

Jules Oppert [4]) was the first Assyriologist to devote himself to the study of neo-babylonian business docu-

1) The earliest text belonging to this class, published in VS (= *Vorderasiatische Schriftdenkmäler*; cf. p. X note 4) V, 1 is written in the year 681 B. C., the latest, published by Strassmaier in *Zeitschrift für Assyriologie* III, p. 147 is written in the year 80 B. C. Before Sennacherib, there is a large gap in Babylonian contract-literature, no clay-tablets having been found belonging to the time between Kaštiliaš II (about 1250 B. C.) and Sennacherib (705—681 B. C.).

2) By Nabopolassar (625 B. C.), the founder of the Chaldaean empire.

3) Texts belonging to the time of the Assyrian supremacy are rather scarce and have not been included in the present collection.

4) Cf. especially *Documents Juridiques de l'Assyrie et de la Chaldée par M.M. Oppert et J. Ménant* (Paris 1877).

ments [1]). But since only a comparatively small number of such texts were at his disposal, many difficulties remained unsolved. The first publication of a large collection was undertaken by J. N. STRASSMAIER who, in the year 1885, edited 181 documents of the neobabylonian period [2]). The greater part of this collection he re-edited in an elaborate series (1887—1897) in which he published altogether about 3000 neobabylonian business documents [3]). An exhaustive study of the first volumes of this work led F. E. PEISER to the publication of similar texts of the Berlin Museum [4]). PEISER laid the foundation for the interpretation of neo-babylonian business documents by furnishing, in addition to the autograph copies, a complete transliteration and

1) In this summary only the more important works and treatises are enumerated.

2) J. N. STRASSMAIER, *Die babylonischen Inschriften im Museum zu Liverpool nebst anderen aus der Zeit von Nebukadnezzar bis Darius.* (Actes du VIe Congrès International des Orientalistes, Vol. II, p. 519 ff). Leide 1885.

3) *Babylonische Texte.* Heft I—IV. *Inschriften von Nabonidus, König von Babylon.* (Leipzig 1887—1889.) Heft V—VI. *Inschriften von Nabuchodonozor, König von Babylon.* (Leipzig 1889.) Heft VII. *Inschriften von Cyrus, König von Babylon.* (Leipzig 1890.) Heft VIII—IX. *Inschriften von Cambyses, König von Babylon.* (Leipzig 1890.) Heft X—XII. *Inschriften von Darius, König von Babylon.* (Leipzig 1893—1897, incomplete). The texts belonging to the reign of the kings between Nebuchadrezzar and Nabonidus have been edited in the same series (*Babylonische Texte,* Heft VI[B]) by B. T. A. EVETTS, *Inscriptions of the Reigns of Evil-Merodach, Neriglissar and Laborosoarchod.* (Leipzig 1892.)

4) F. E. PEISER, *Keilschriftliche Actenstücke aus Babylonischen Städten.* (Berlin 1889) and F. E. PEISER, *Babylonische Verträge des Berliner Museums.* (Berlin 1890.)

translation, as well as a commentary to the texts.

At about the same time K. L. TALLQVIST [1]) compiled a glossary containing the words of the texts which up to that time had been published by STRASSMAIER, while, in addition to his former treatises, F.E. PEISER published a collection of selected transliterated and translated texts in the 4th volume of E. SCHRADER's *Keilinschriftliche Bibliothek* [2]). In collaboration with Professor KOHLER of Berlin, he also issued a valuable series of studies entitled „*Aus dem Babylonischen Rechtsleben*" [3]) in which the business documents are arranged according to their juridical contents. Other treatises based upon STRASSMAIER's texts are those of ZEHNPFUND [4]), DEMUTH [5]), ZIEMER [6]) and MARX [7]).

New material was furnished by the excavations of Messrs. PETERS and HAYNES at Nippur for the Univer-

---

1) K. L. TALLQVIST, *Die Sprache der Kontrakte Nabû-nâ'ids.* (Helsingfors 1890).

2) F. E. PEISER, *Texte juristischen und geschäftlichen Inhalts* (*Keilinschriftliche Bibliothek*, Band IV). Berlin 1896.

3) J. KOHLER u. F. E. PEISER, *Aus dem Babylonischen Rechtsleben*, I—IV. (Leipzig 1890—1898).

4) R. ZEHNPFUND, *Babylonische Weberrechnungen* (*Beiträge zur Assyriologie und vergleichenden semitischen Sprachwissenschaft* [abbrev. BA] I, p. 492 ff.). Leipzig 1890.

5) L. DEMUTH, *Fünfzig Rechts- und Verwaltungsurkunden aus der Zeit des Königs Kyros* (BA III, p. 393 ff.). Leipzig 1898. Cf. also F. DELITZSCH's remarks (*Notizen zu den neubabylonischen Kontrakttafeln*) in BA III, p. 385 ff.

6) E. ZIEMER, *Fünfzig Rechts- und Verwaltungsurkunden aus der Zeit des Königs Kambyses* (BA III, p. 445 ff.). Leipzig 1898.

7) V. MARX, *Die Stellung der Frauen in Babylonien gemäss den Kontrakten aus der Zeit von Nebukadnezar bis Darius* (BA IV, 1 ff.) Leipzig 1902.

sity of Pennsylvania. This material was published in three volumes with splendid autograph plates by A. T. CLAY [1]).

The names contained in the neo-babylonian business documents, excepting those published by the Pennsylvania University [2]), have been collected and explained by K. L. TALLQVIST [3]). The neo-babylonian business documents preserved in the Berlin Museum have been published by the present writer in the „*Vorderasiatische Schriftdenkmäler*" [4]) III—VI.

The present collection of neo-babylonian business documents has, in accordance with the general purposes of the Semitic Study Series, been prepared primarily for the use of beginners. This will justify occasional emendations and restorations of corrupt and defective

1) The first volume was issued under the title H. V. HILPRECHT and A. T. CLAY, *Business Documents of Murashû Sons of Nippur, dated in the reign of Artaxerxes I (The Babylonian Expedition of the University of Pennsylvania*, Series A, Vol. IX). Philadelphia 1898; the second as A. T. CLAY, *Business Documents of Murashû Sons of Nippur, dated in the reign of Darius II* (ib. Series A, Vol. X). Philadelphia 1904; the third as A. T. CLAY, *Legal and Commercial Transactions dated in the Assyrian, Neo-Babylonian and Persian Periods chiefly from Nippur* (ib. Series A, Vol. VIII, 1). Philadelphia 1908. To the 1st vol. Prof. HILPRECHT contributed the introduction and concordance of proper names and also copied a number of the texts.

2) These were not incorporated into TALLQVIST's book, because separate lists had been given by the authors.

3) K. L. TALLQVIST, *Neubabylonisches Namenbuch (Acta Societatis Scientiarum Fennicae* Tom. XXXII). Helsingfors 1905.

4) *Vorderasiatische Schriftdenkmäler des Berliner Museums, herausgegeben von der Generalverwaltung*, Heft III—IV (Leipzig 1907); Heft V—VI (Leipzig 1908).

passages. In every case, the original edition of the texts can be consulted by means of the following concordance.

1 = Nd [1] 541	18 = Nd 535	35 = Nk 100
2 = VS [2] IV 15	19 = Nd 614	36 = Nd 665
3 = VS IV 38	20 = Nd 821	37 = Nk 70
4 = Ngl [3] 39	21 = Nd 420	38 = Nd 392
5 = Nk [4] 91	22 = Nk 325	39 = Nd 832
6 = Ngl 69	23 = Nd 788	40 = Nd 340
7 = VS IV 10	24 = Nd 925	41 = Nd 116
8 = Nd 372	25 = Nk 28	42 = Nk 164
9 = Nd 133	26 = Nd 745	43 = Nk 101
10 = VS IV 53	27 = Nd 2	44 = Nd 243
11 = Nd 270	28 = Nd 522	45 = Nd 348
12 = Nk 320	29 = Nd 256	46 = Nd 697
13 = Nd 921	30 = Nk 145	47 = Nk 368
14 = VS III 58	31 = Nd 208	48 = Nk 365
15 = Nd 819	32 = Nd 184	49 = Nk 342
16 — Nd 47	33 = Ngl 52	50 = Nd 13
17 = Nd 1008	34 = Nd 1019	

Berlin, Easter 1908. A. UNGNAD.

1) Nd = STRASSMAIER, *Inschriften von Nabonidus*, v. p. VIII, note 3,

2) Vs = *Vorderasiatische Schriftdenkmäler*, v. p. X, note 4.

3) Ngl = EVETTS, *Inscriptions* etc., v. p. VIII, note 3.

4) Nk = STRASSMAIER, *Inschriften von Nabuchodonosor*, v. p. VIII. note 3.

1.

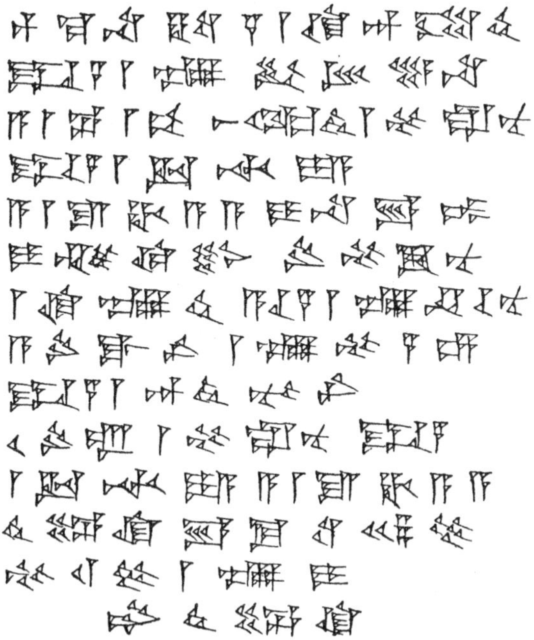

2.

3.

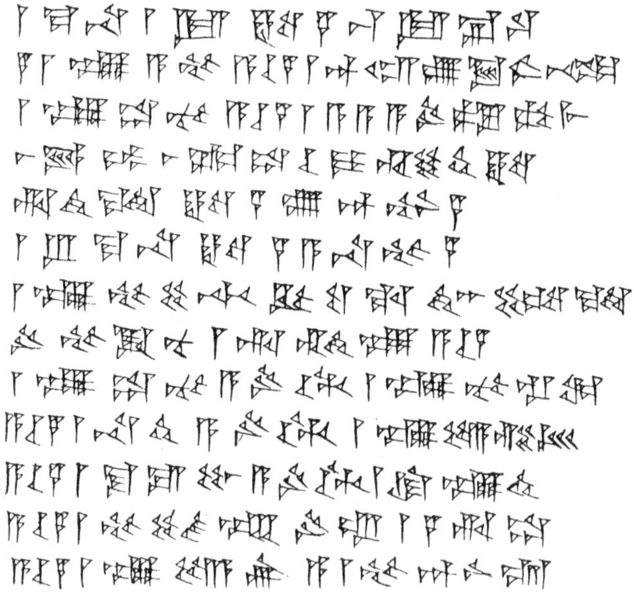

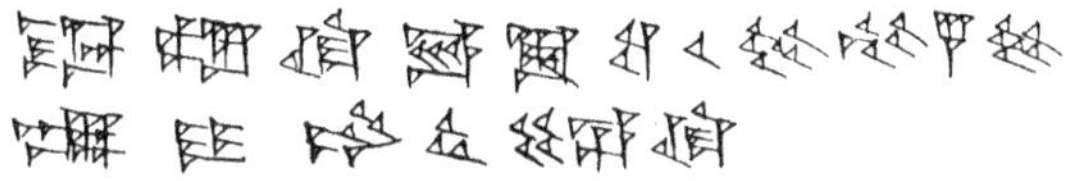

4.

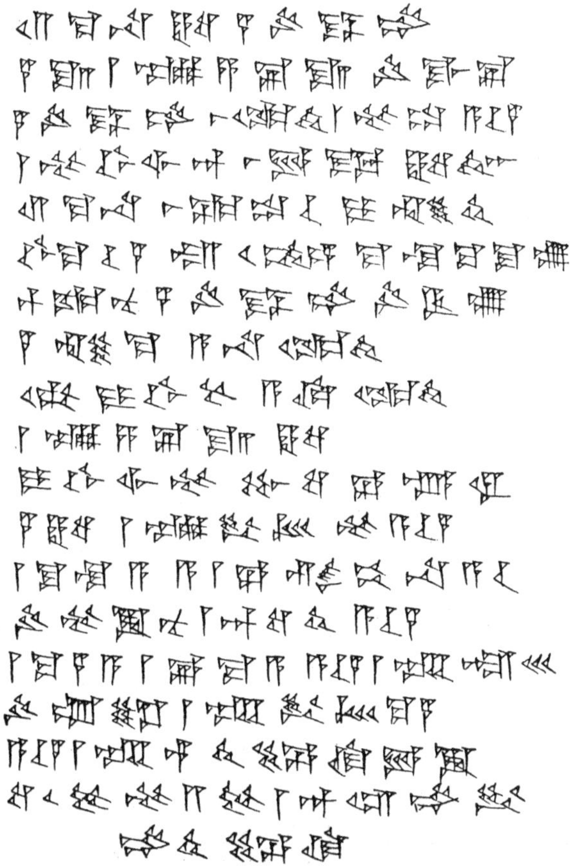

5.

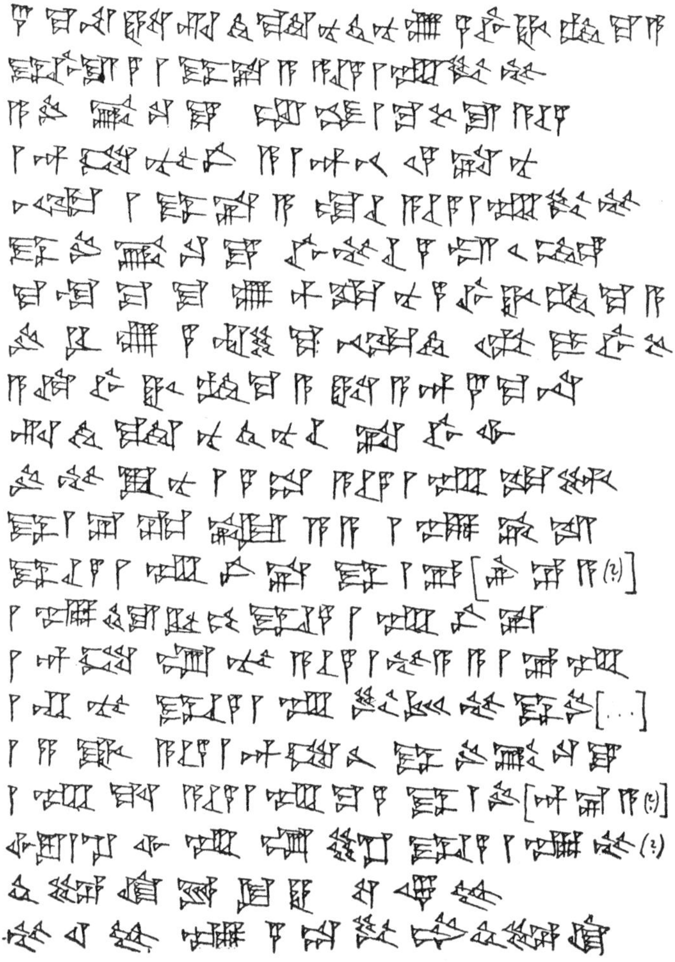

6.

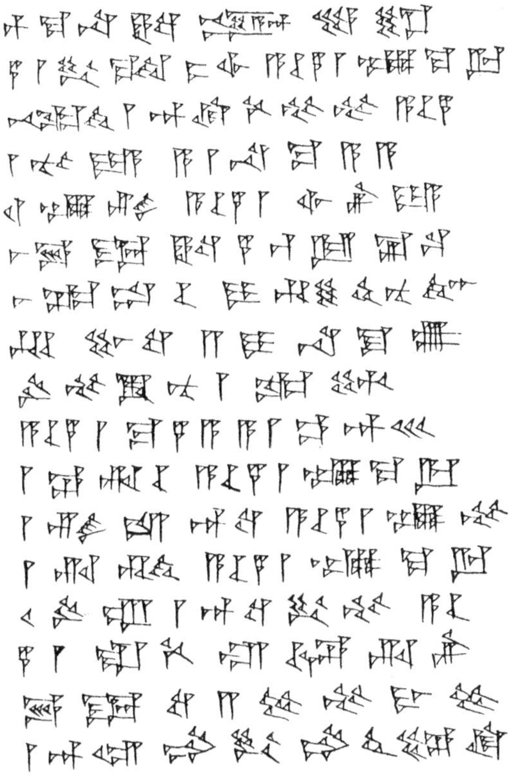

7.

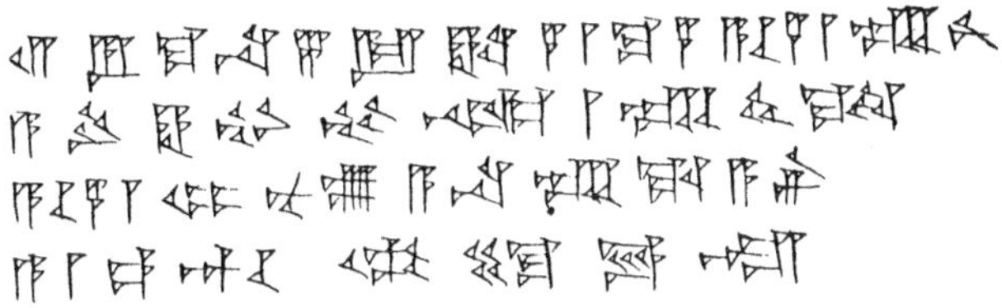

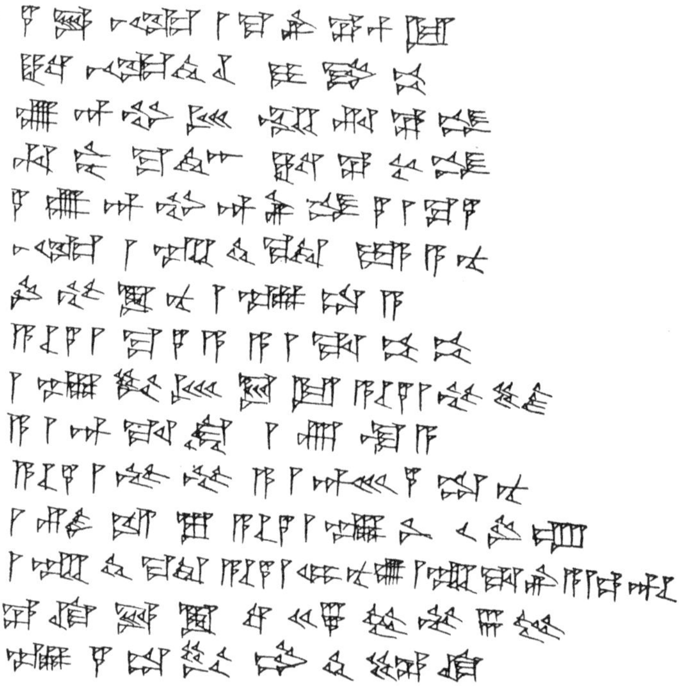

8.

[illegible]
[illegible]
[illegible]
[illegible]
[illegible]
[illegible]
[illegible]

9.

[illegible]
[illegible]
[illegible]
[illegible]
[illegible]
[illegible]
[illegible]
[illegible]
[illegible]
[illegible]
[illegible]
[illegible]
[illegible]

10

[illegible]

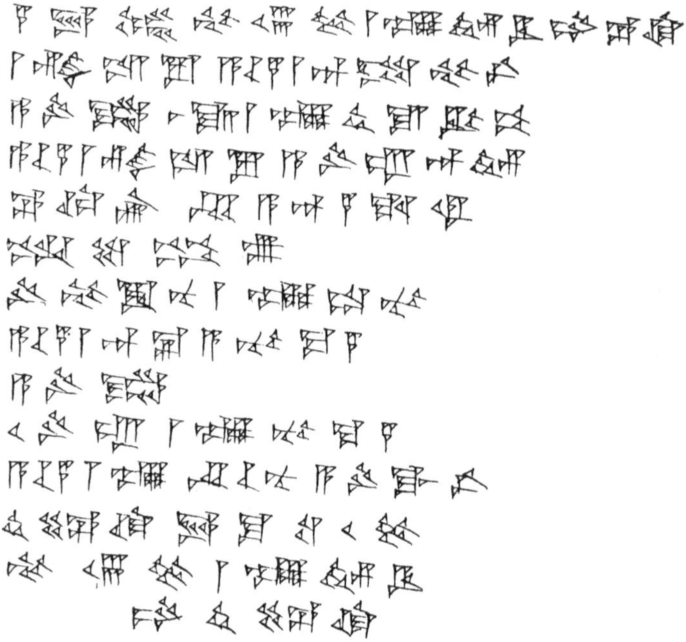

11.

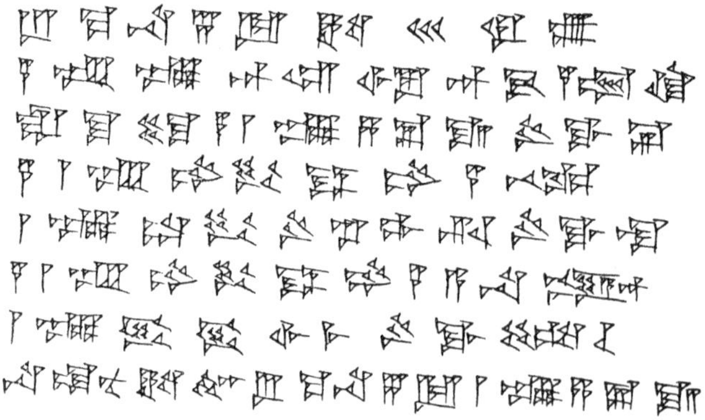

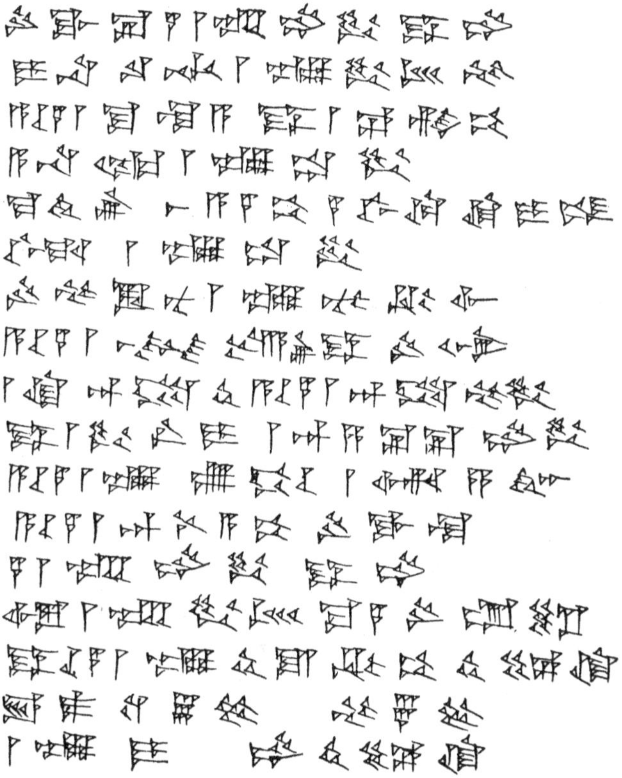

12.

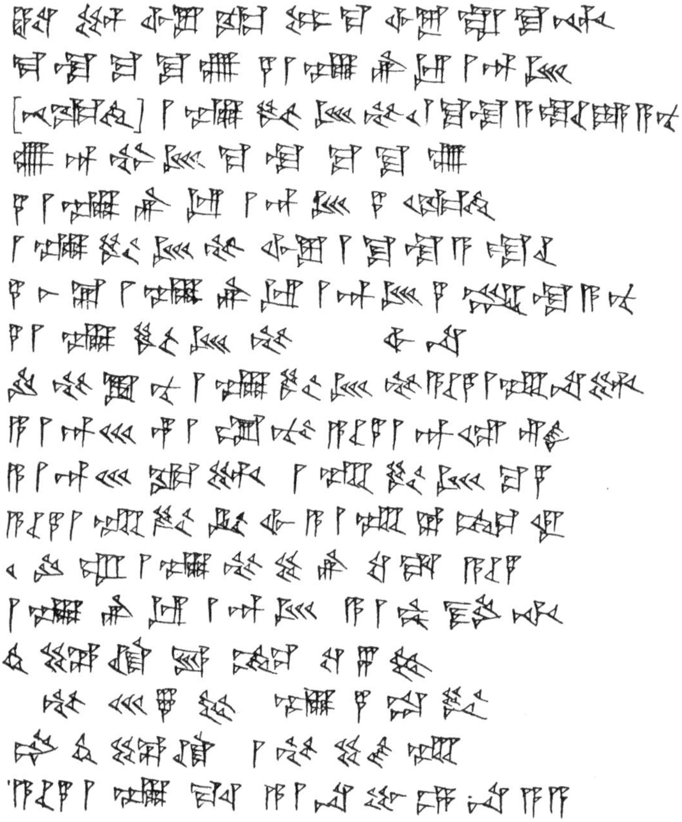

13.

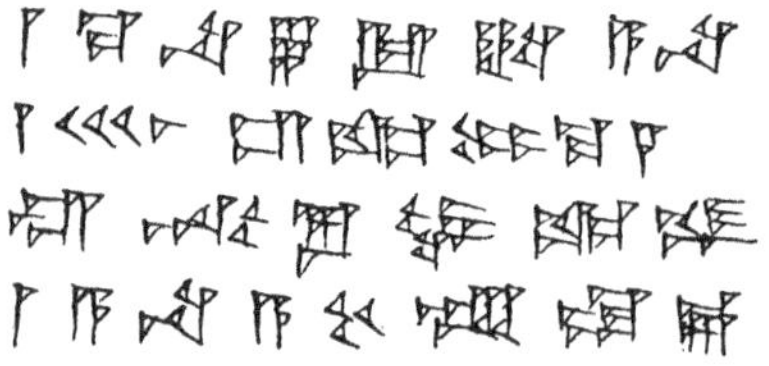

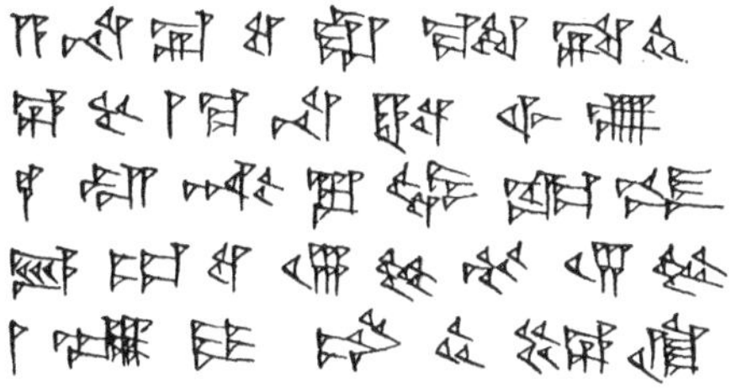

14.

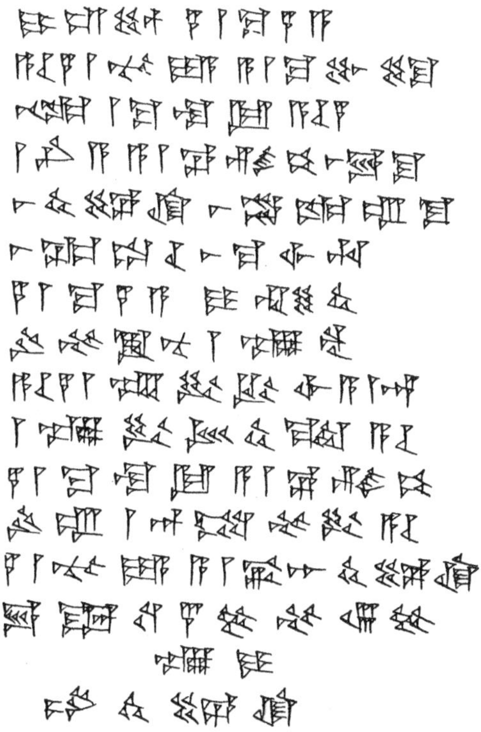

15.

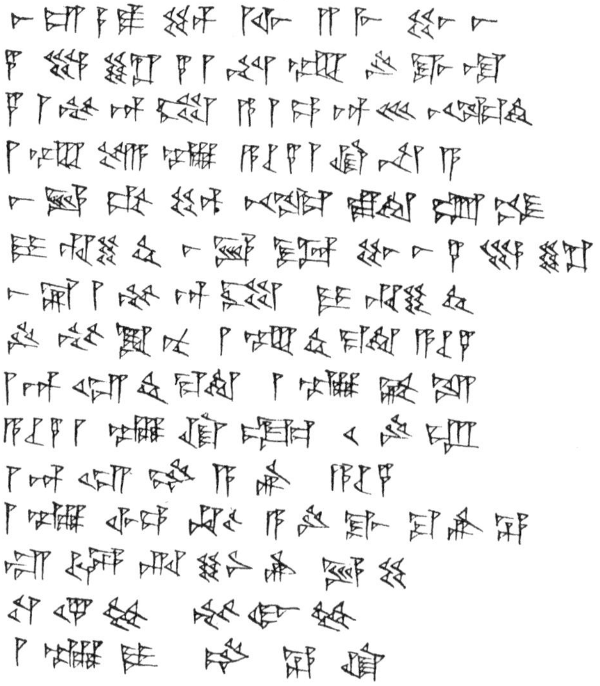

16.

[illegible]
[illegible]
[illegible]
[illegible]
[illegible]
[illegible]
[illegible]
[illegible]

17.

[illegible]
[illegible]
[illegible]
[illegible]
[illegible]
[illegible]
[illegible]
[illegible]
[illegible]
[illegible]
[illegible]
[illegible]
[illegible]
[illegible]

18.

19.

20.

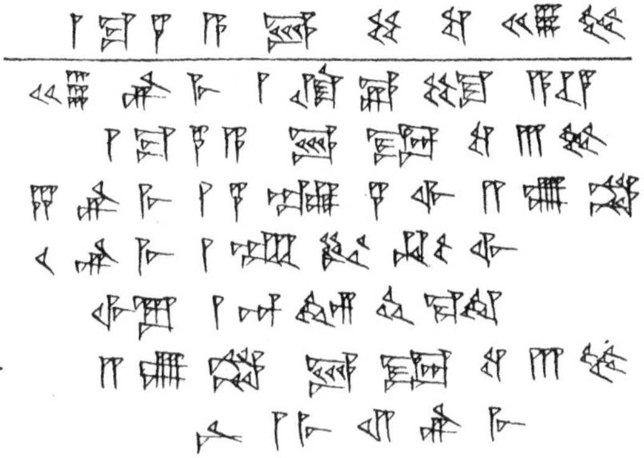

21.

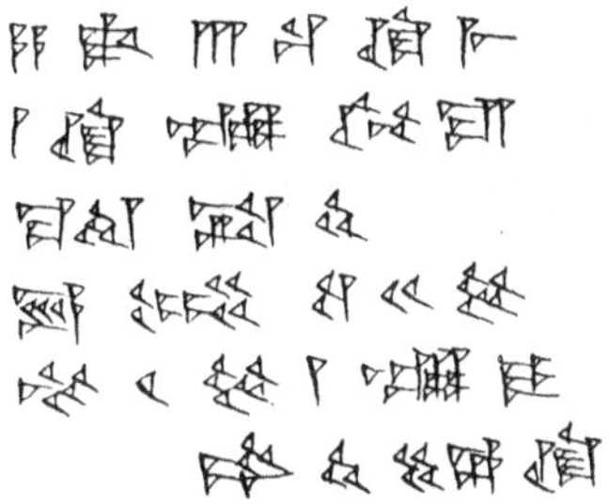

22.

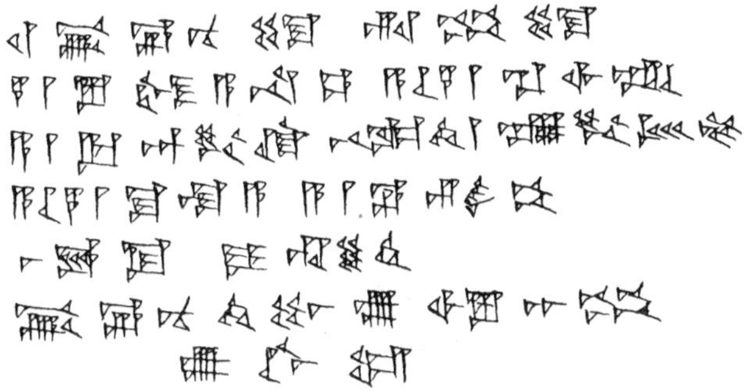

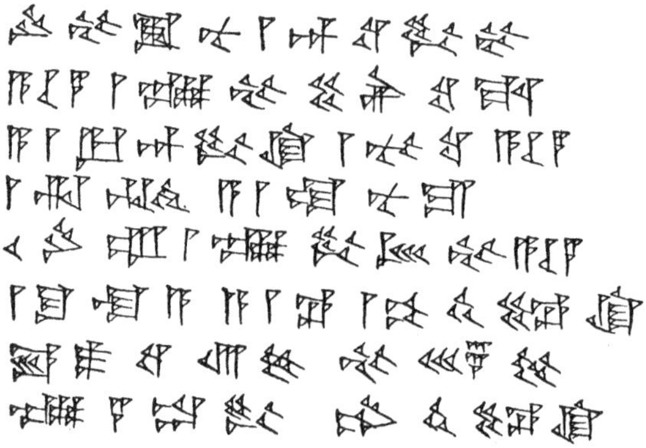

23.

24.

25.

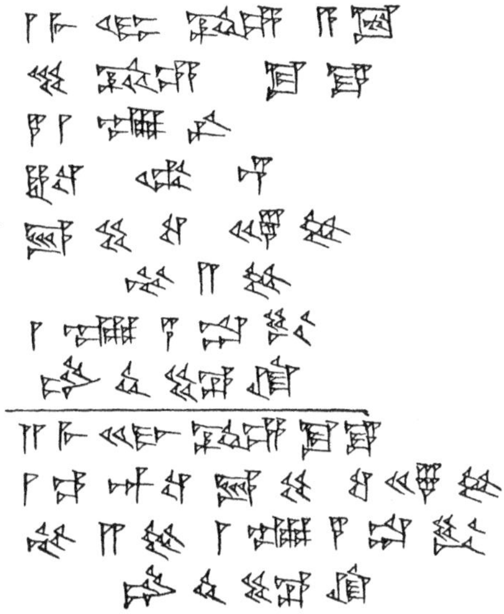

26.

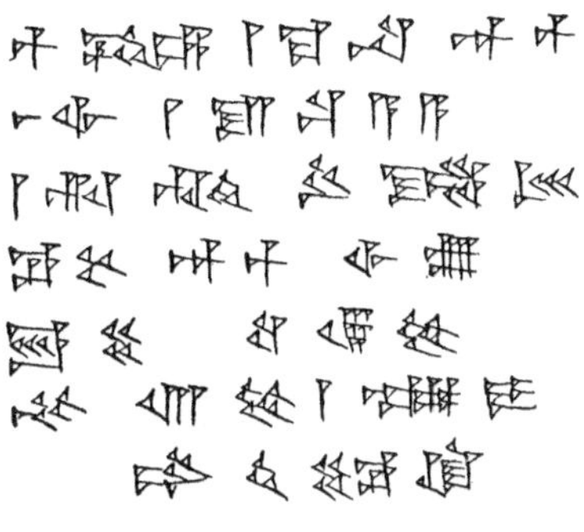

27.

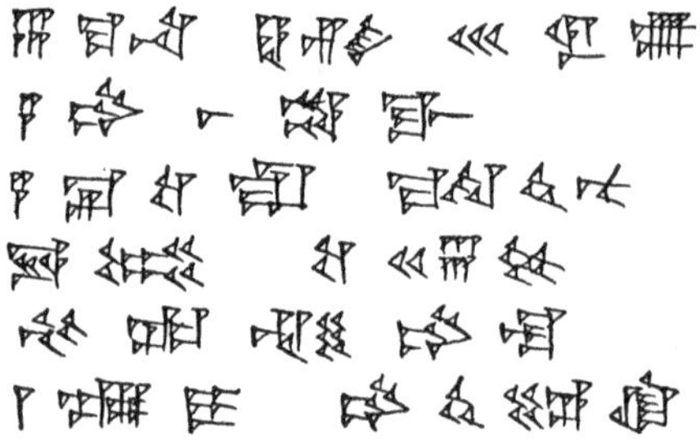

28.

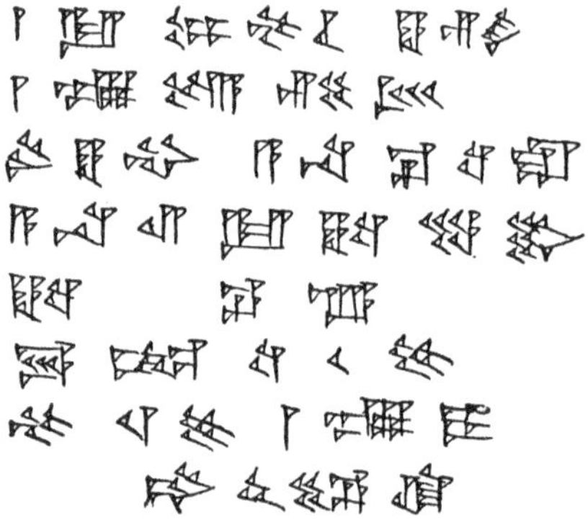

29.

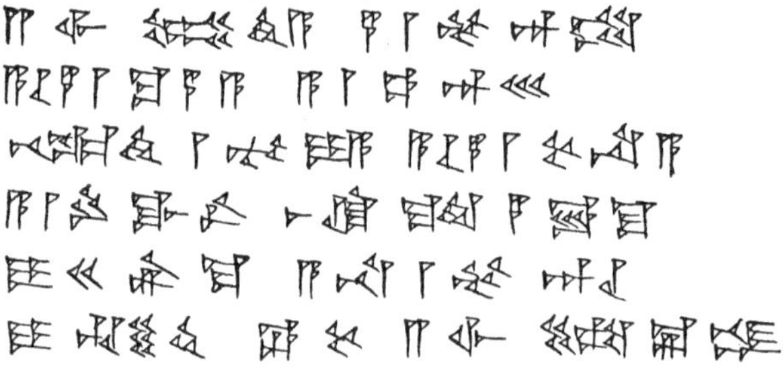

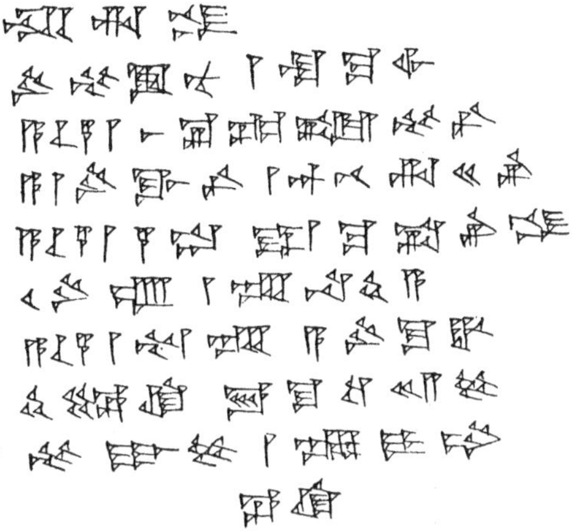

30

31.

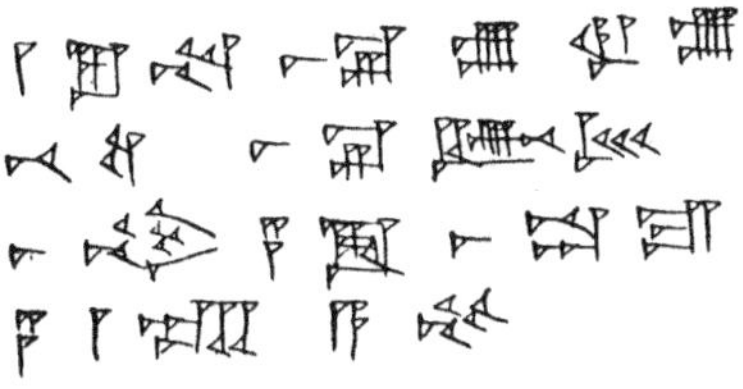

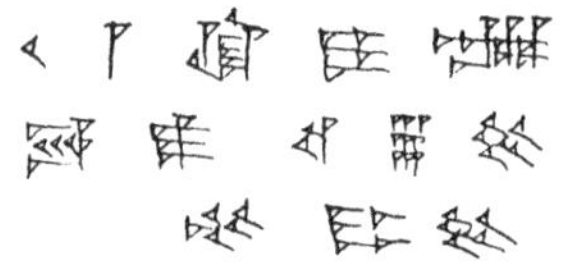

32

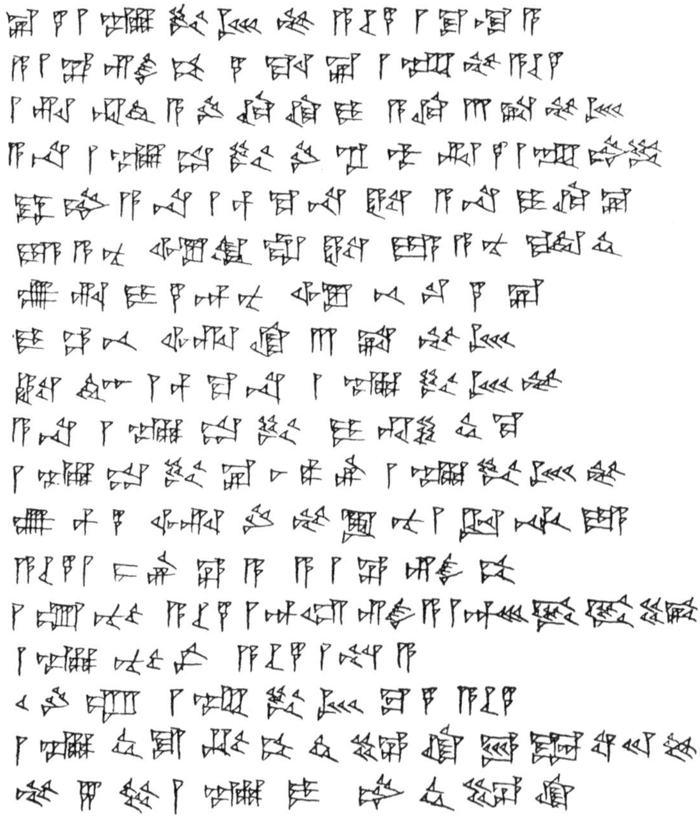

33.

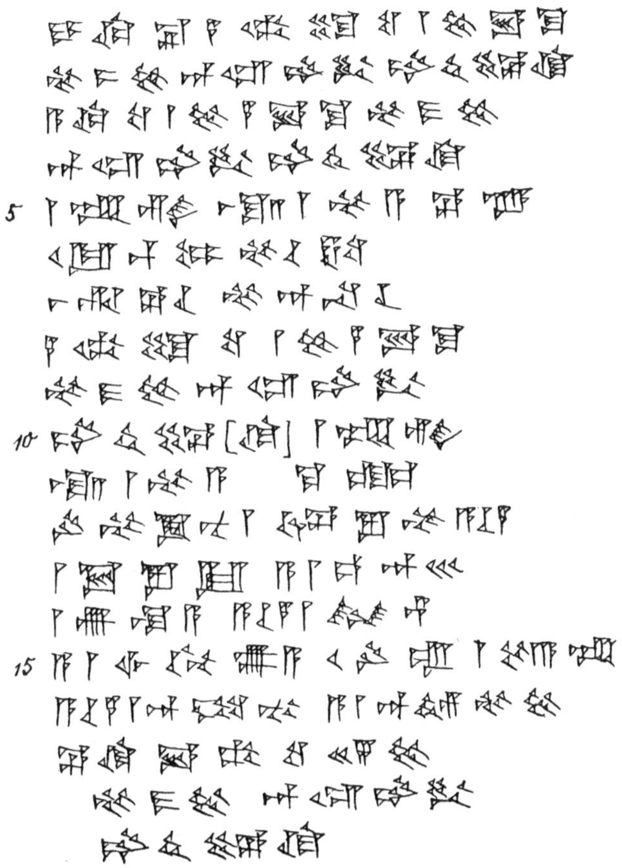

34.

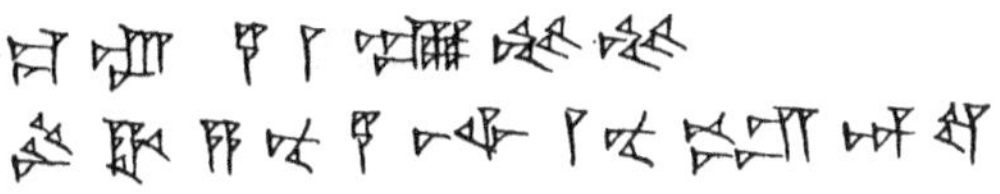

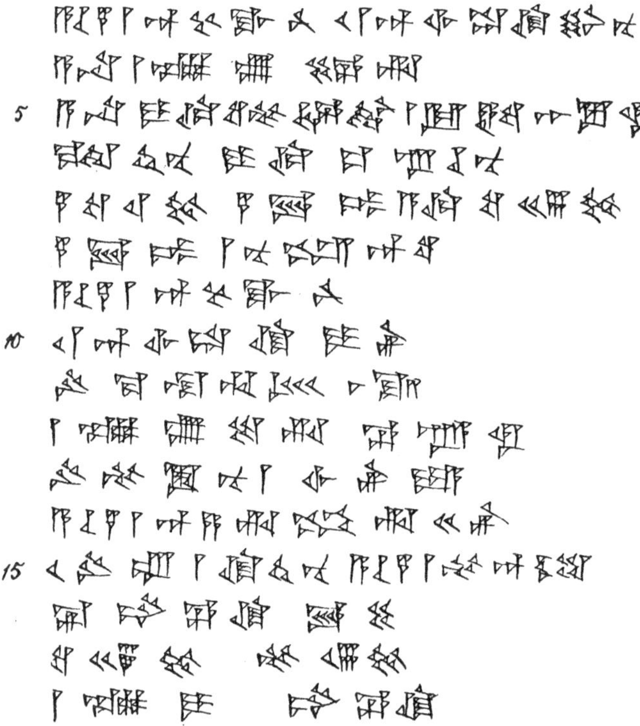

35.

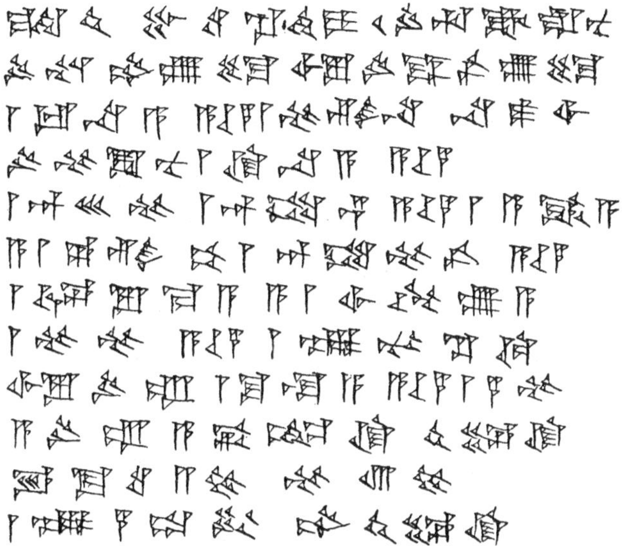

36.

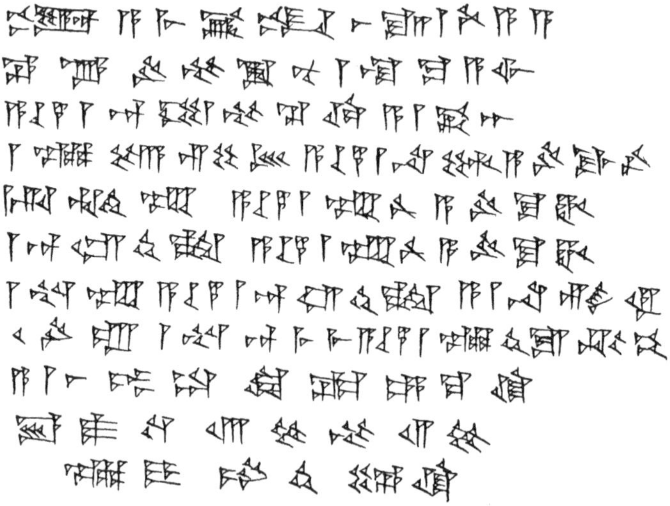

37.

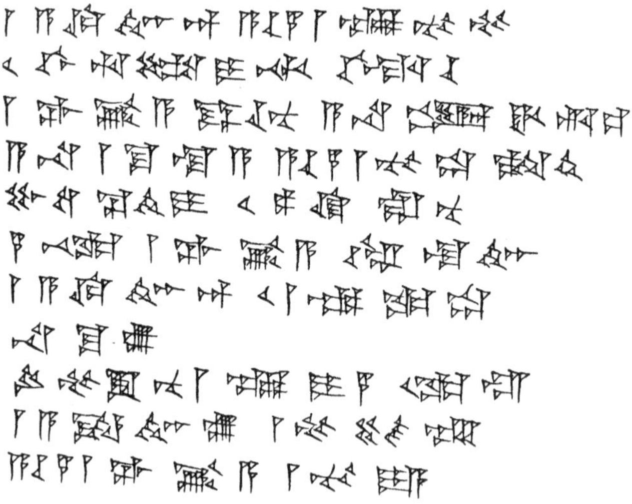

38.

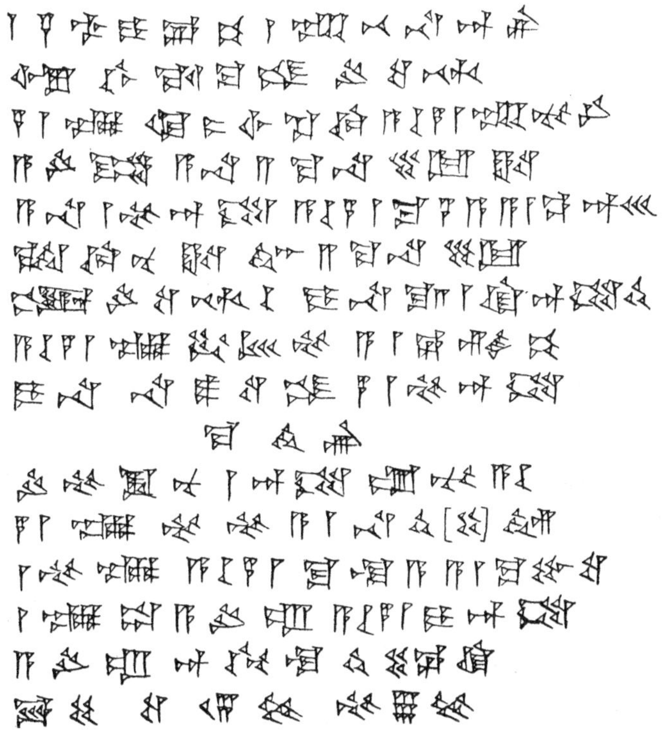

39.

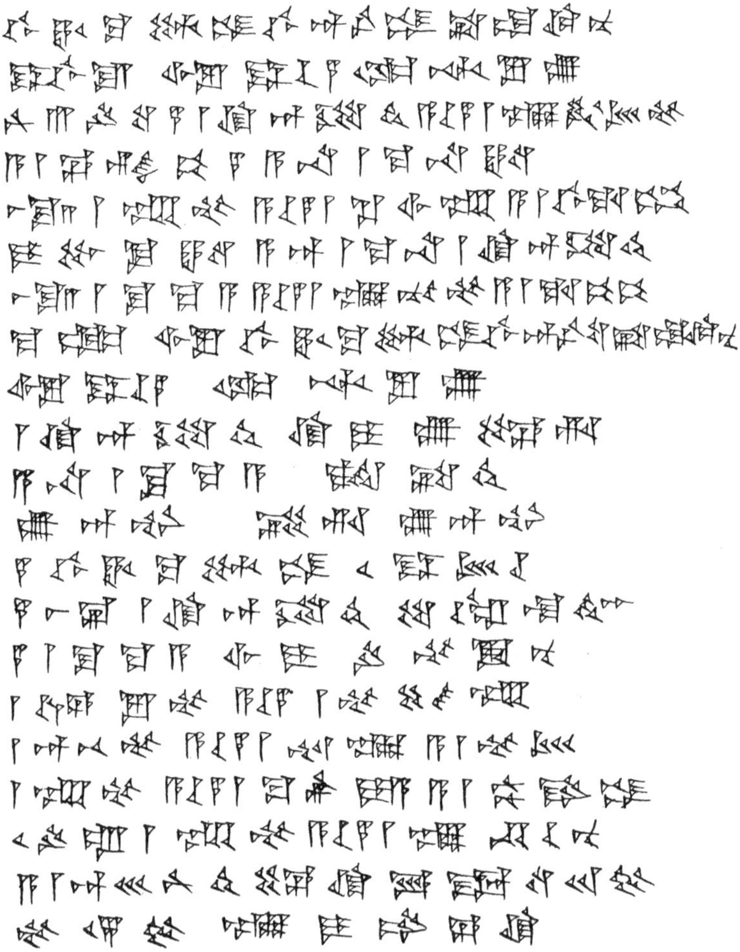

40.

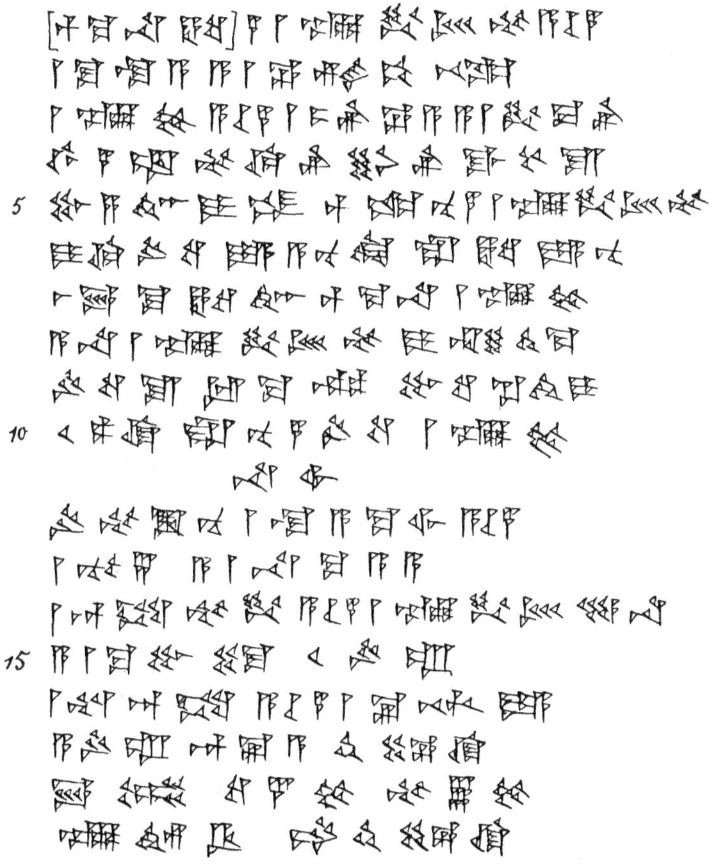

41.

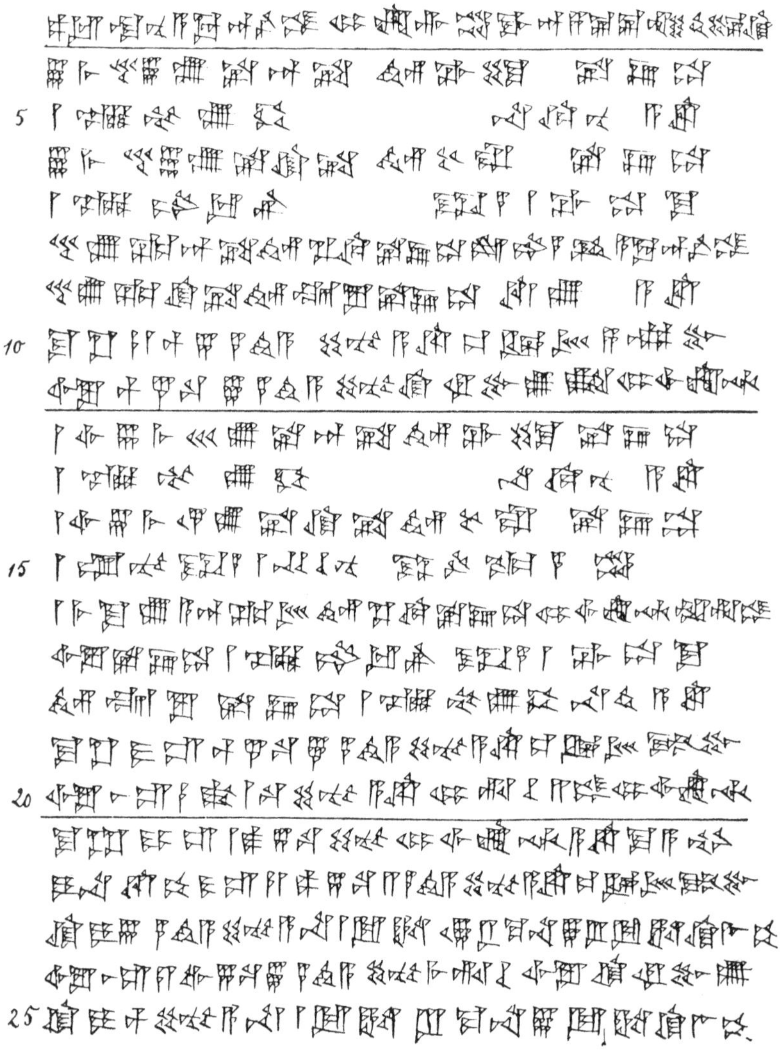

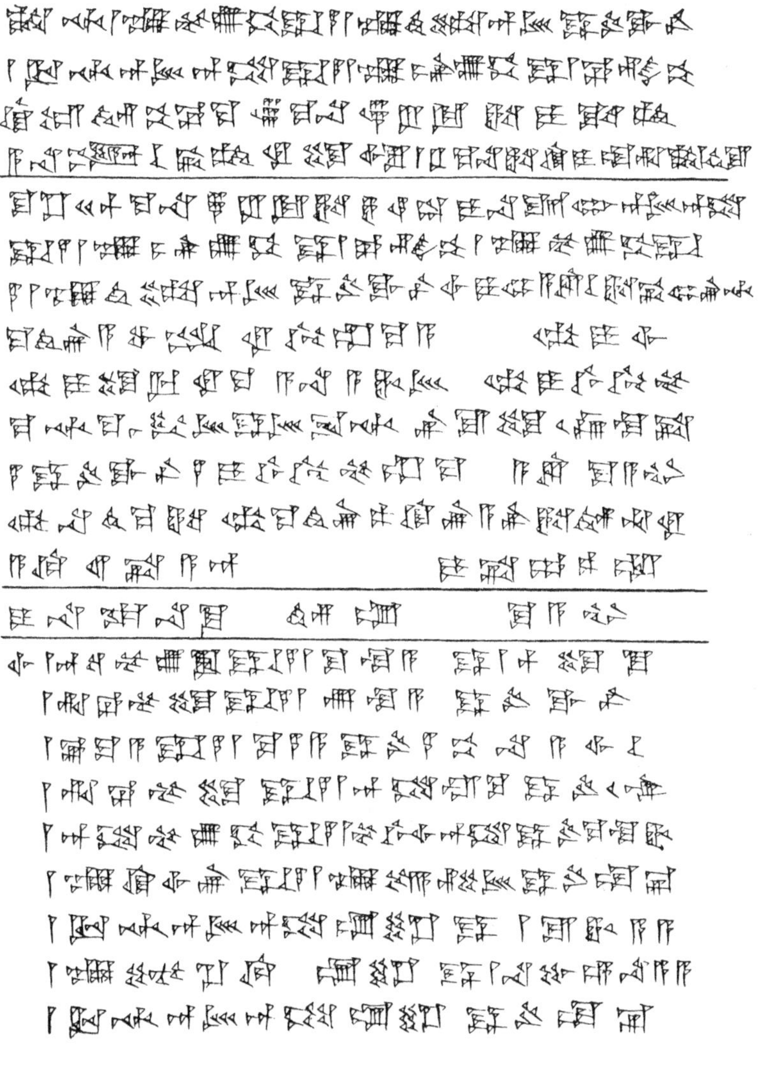

42.

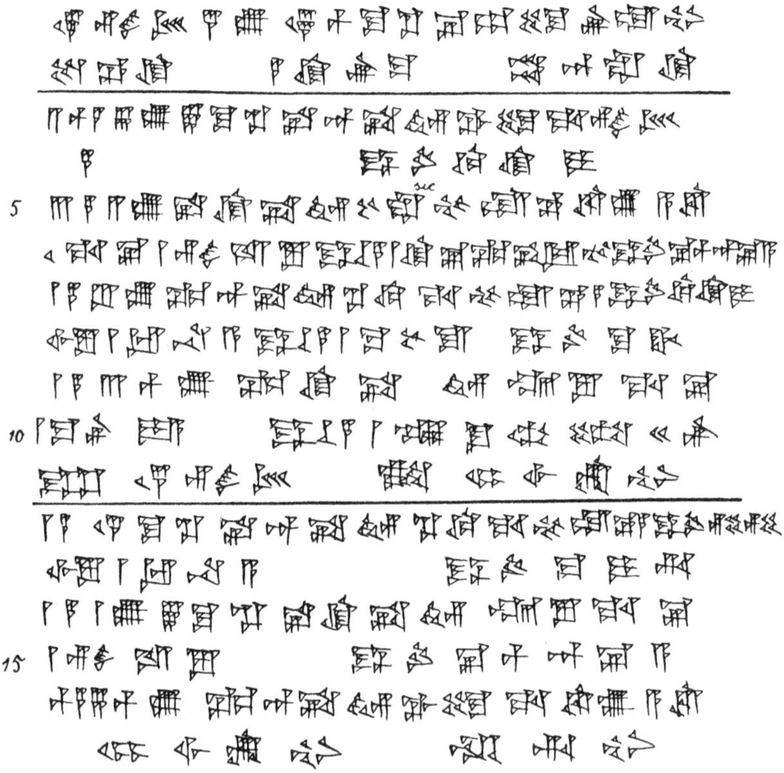

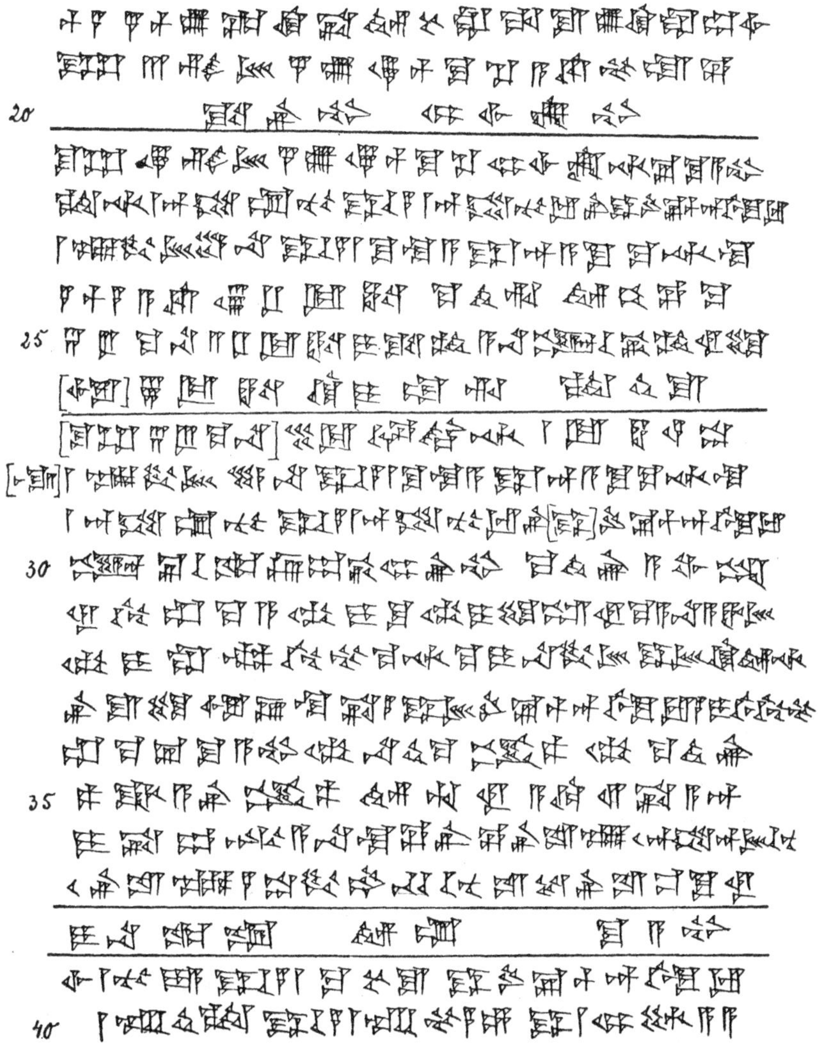

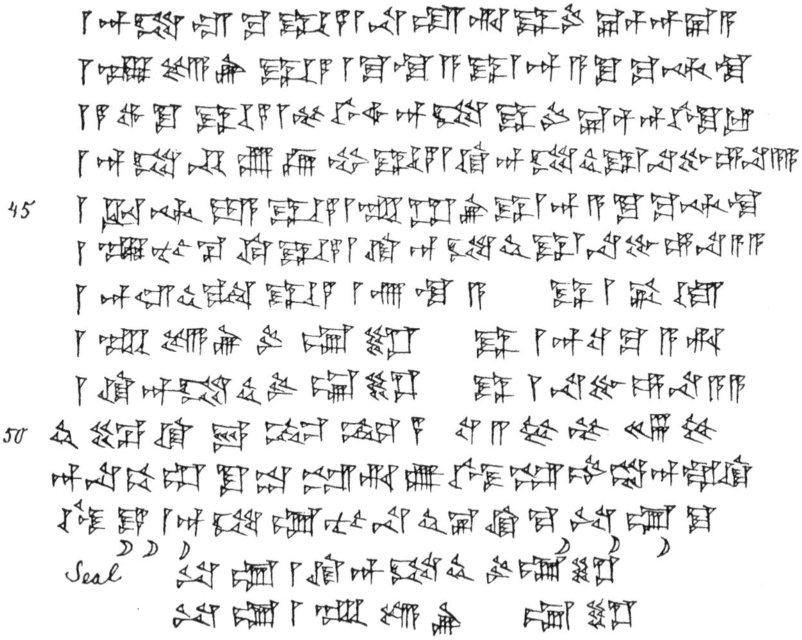

43.

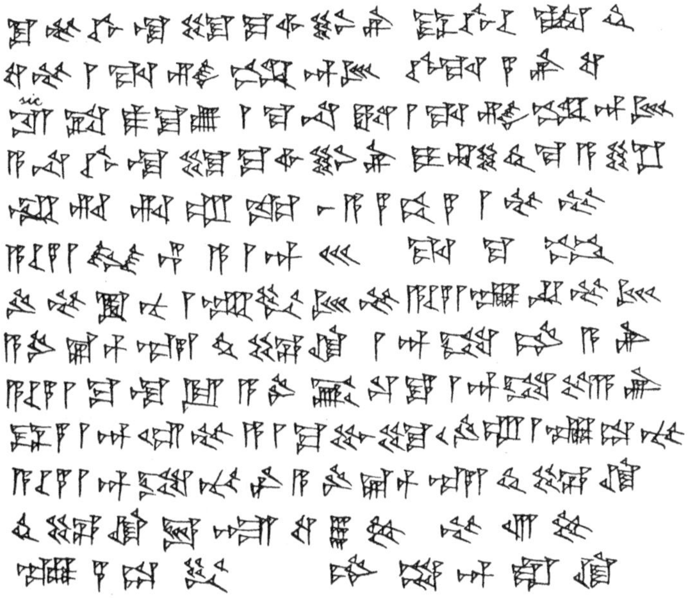

44.

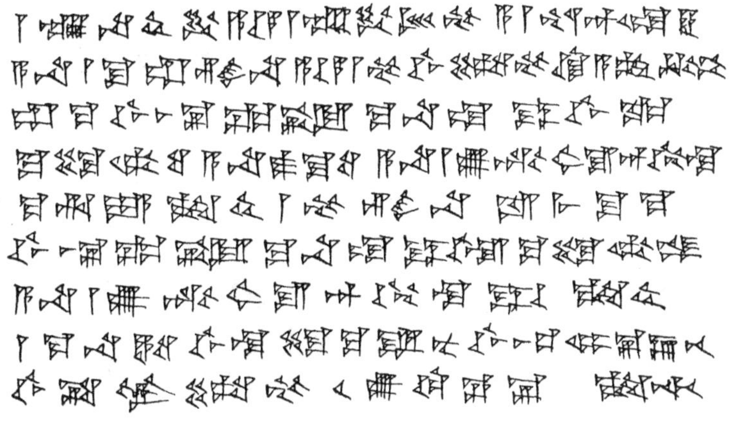

45.

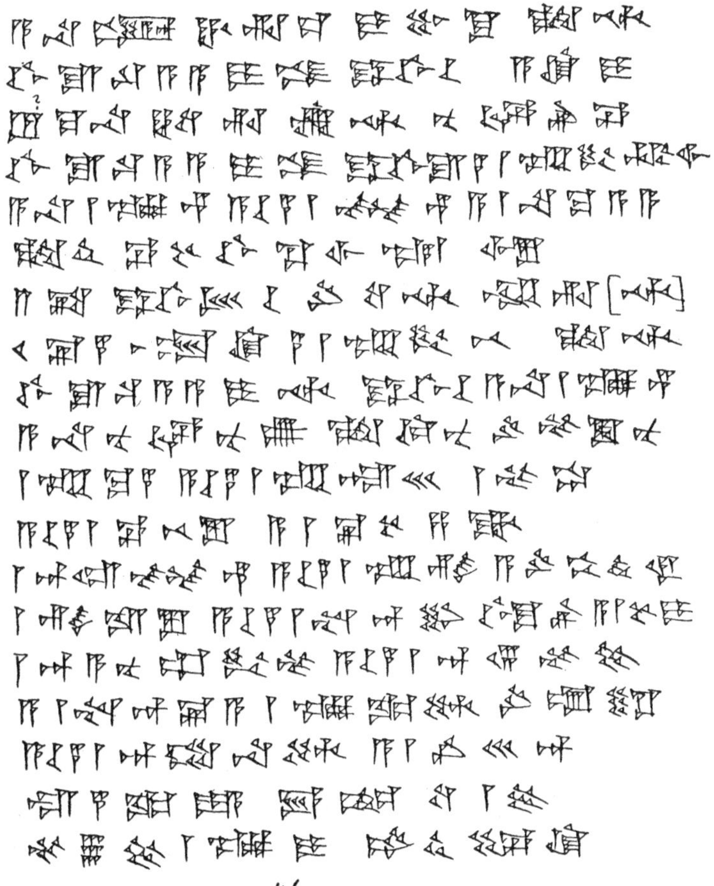

46.

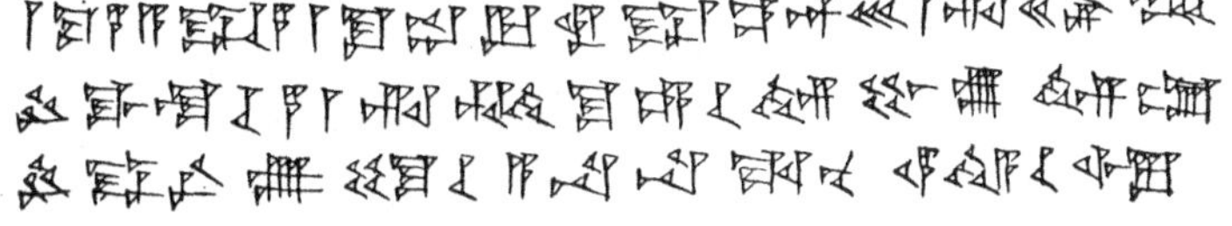

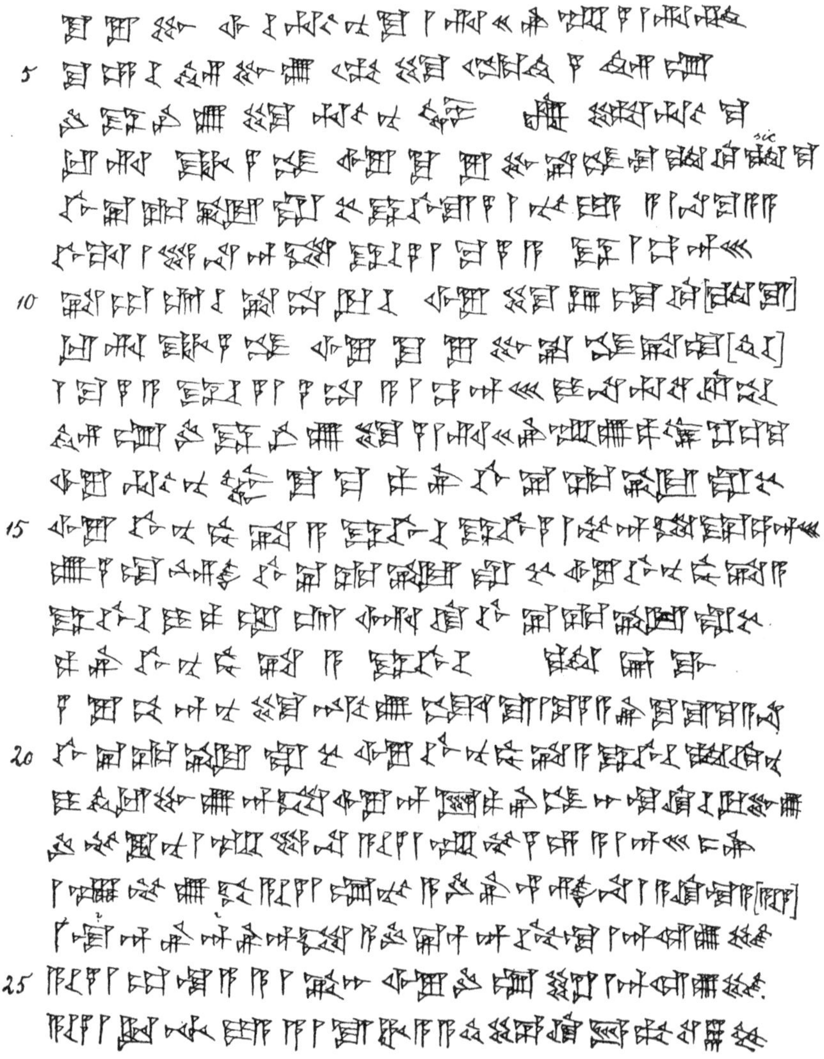

47.

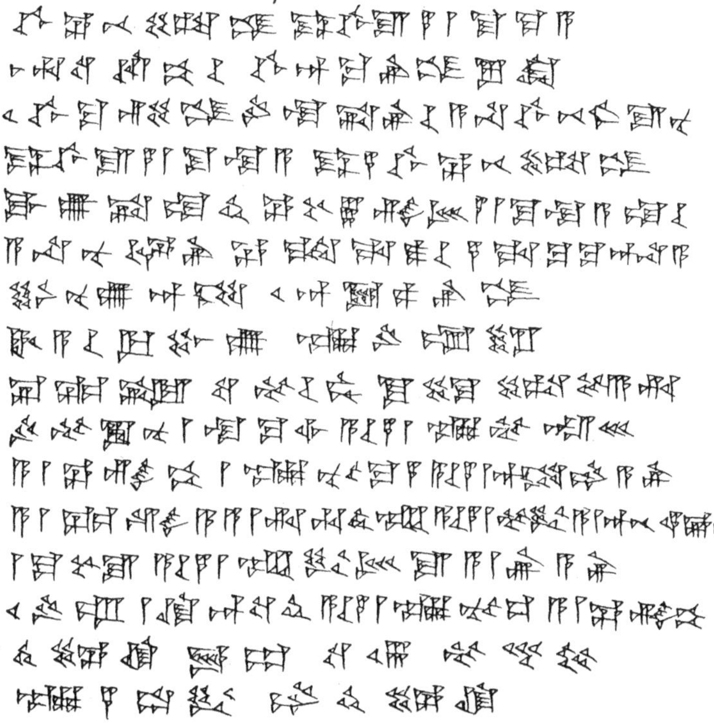

48.

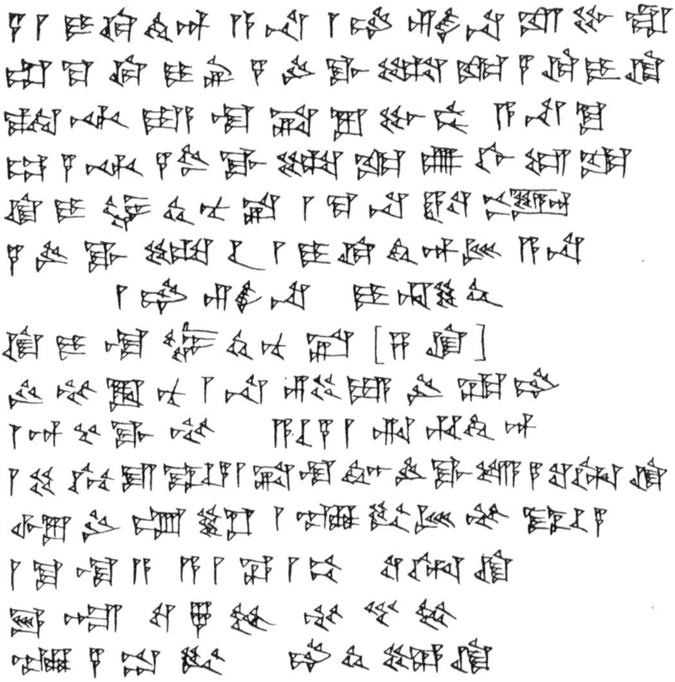

49.

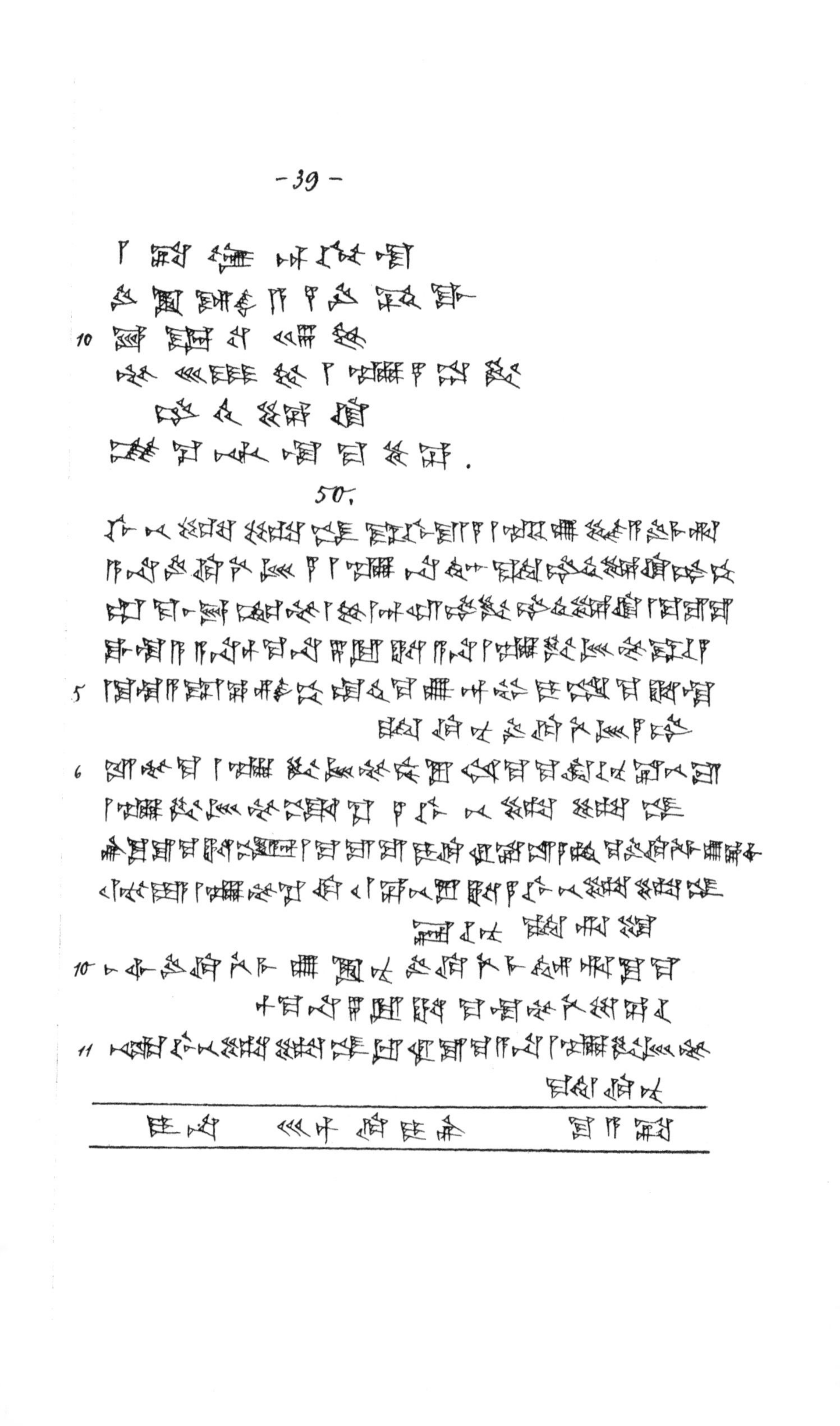

[illegible]
[illegible]
10 [illegible]
[illegible]
[illegible]
[illegible]

50.

[illegible]
[illegible]
[illegible]
[illegible]
5 [illegible]
[illegible]
6 [illegible]
[illegible]
[illegible]
[illegible]
[illegible]
10 [illegible]
[illegible]
11 [illegible]
[illegible]

[illegible]

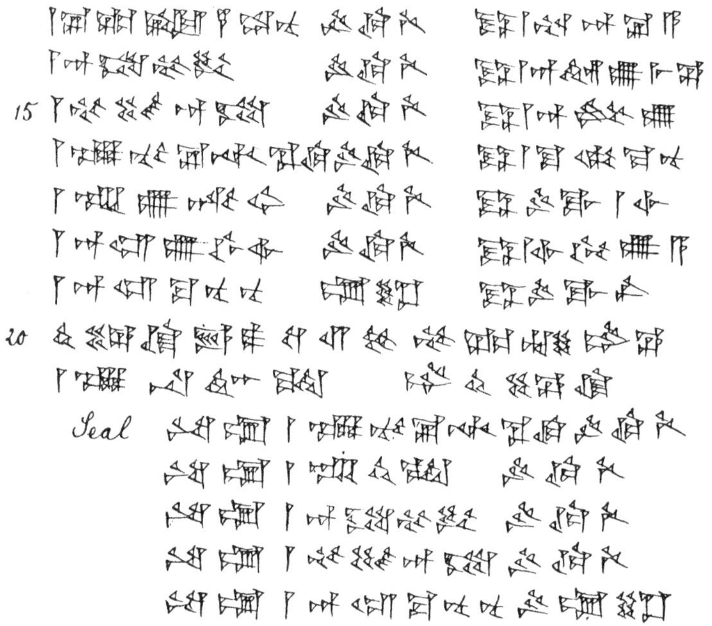

Measures &c

[cuneiform] (1 gurru) = 5 [cuneiform] ; [cuneiform] (1 PI) = 36 [cuneiform]

[cuneiform] (1 ḲA) = 10 [cuneiform] ; [cuneiform] (1 GAR) = 2 [cuneiform] (ḳanû);

[cuneiform] (1 ḳanû) = 7 [cuneiform] (ammatu); 1 [cuneiform] = 24 [cuneiform] (ubânu).

[cuneiform] = 6 ḲA ; [cuneiform] = 12 ḲA ; [cuneiform] = 18 ḲA ; [cuneiform] = 24 ḲA ; [cuneiform] = 30 ḲA.

[cuneiform] (1 biltu) = 60 [cuneiform] ; [cuneiform] (manû) = 60 [cuneiform] (šiḳlu).

[cuneiform] = 1 PI ; [cuneiform] = 2 PI ; [cuneiform] = 3 PI ; [cuneiform] = 4 PI

List of signs.

1	aš, dil; ina, ištên		Marduk
2	ḫal		NIN.IB (אנושת)
3	êreš (ארש)		Šulmânu
4	bal, pal; innû (אני)		Pârisu (?)
5	an, il; ilu		Amurru
	Ea		Nabû
	parzillu; NIN.IB (אנושת)		Bêl
	Nanna(r)		Ištar
	Bau	6	muḳ
	Nabû	7	ag, ak, aḳ
	elû	8	er; âlu (also determ.)
	Bêlit	9	maḫ
	Nergal	10	la
	Marduk	11	nu; ul
	Nergal	12	zêru
	Nergal	13	pap; napḫaru, nâṣir, uṣur (נצר).
	Ištar		
	Sin	14	gil
	Šamaš	15	ardu
	Ašur	16	^{aban}kunukku
	Addu	17	ḳa; ḲA (a measure)
	Gula	18	kâṣir (כצר)

19 be, bad, bat, pit, til, ziz; mîtu, ušabši (בשר)

20 ti

21 tim

22 ṭâbtu

23 mu; šumu; nâdin, iddin(a) (נדן)

šattu

šumâti (= šu'âti)

24 aḫu; uṣur (נצר)

25 amêlu; determ. before names of professions

26 na

27 maš; mišlu; 6 ḲA

28 ik, iḳ; ušabši (בשי)

29 ḫu

30 nam; piḫâtu

(or) šarrûtu

31 mut

32 = + išten[en]

33 si; cf. 81

34 rat

35 ri, tal

36 zi; napištu

dikû

37 gi; ḳanû; (m)ušallim (שלם)

ginû; ukîn (כון)

38 en; bêlu

39 ṣil

abkallu

40 šur, êṭir, eṭir (אטר)

41 bânû, bânî, ibnî (בני); îpuš, êpeš (אפש)

42 ni, tiḳ

amel NI.ŠUR

43 ir

44 tab; 2

45 gan

46 taḳ

47 ab, ap

48 nap

49 um

50 rit; šapik (שפך)

tupšarru

51 Uruk

52	ad, at, aṭ; abu		Addaru (12)
53	ṣi		Addaru arkû (12b)
54	ḳu	63	šarru
55	ur	64	ka; pû
56	Ḫu(m)		suluppu
57	rik	65	naḳ
58	ḳas	66	bi
59	šîmu	67	ub, ar
60	il	68	iš, mil
61	du; nazâzu; (m)ukîn, kîn (כון)	69	bâbu
62	arḫu		abullu, bâbu rabû
	Nisannu (1)		Bâbili
	Ayaru (2)	70	ṭe
	Sîmânu (3)	71	ṣêru
	Du'ûzu (4)	72	ḫaḫ
	Abu (5)	73	pa; 12 ḲA
	Ulûlu (6)	74	is, iṣ; lišir (ישר)
	Tišrîtu (7)		elippu
	Waraḫsamna (8)		ṣillu
	Kislimu (9)		kirû
	Ṭebêtu (10)		gišimmaru
	Šabâṭu (11)	75	pi; PI (meas.)

No.	Reading
	v. 18
76	alpu
77	am
78	dûru
79	ḫir, šir
80	gur; gurru
81	si; v. 33
	lišir (ישר)
82	mar
83	sag; rêšu, pûtu
	ašaridu (?)
	ḳaḳḳadu
84	šap
85	sip; rêû
86	uš; šiddu
	išparu
	ṭaḫu
87	al
88	ga
89	gabrû
90	ta; ištu; determ. after numerals
91	malaḫu

No.	Reading
92	a) má
	b) kit
	c) bit, pit, ê; bîtu
	Êsagila
	êkurru
	Êbarru
	šangû
92b	lak
	šangû, tupšarru
93	ummu
94	laḫ, sukkal
95	u, šam; ammatu
96	e
	Bâbili
97	kal, dan, tan, rib, dannu
98	dag
99	duk, lut; karpatu (determ.)
	paḫḫâru
100	sa
101	ṭir, ṭer
102	ṣab; nûru
103	kišâdu

No.	Reading
	Kûtû
	gugallu
104	biltu
105	un, kalam
106	ellatu
107	ḫarrânu
108	i; na'id (נאד)
109	ya
110	kim
111	ba; iḳîša (קיש)
112	ma
	manû
113	aš; 18 ḲA
114	24 ḲA
115	da, ṭa; li'û, iti
116	id, it, iṭ, eṭ
117	zu; îdū (ידא)
118	= + ištît ^{it}
119	(with) nappâḫu
120	mâru
	mârtu
	ablu
121	rab
122	ra
123	zaḳ
	imittu
124	, ḳar
125	šu; ḳâtu
	ubânu
	, etc. napḫaru
	bâ'iru
126	gal, ḳal; rabû
	ḳallu
127	bar
128	ša
129	su; erba (ערב)
130	šin
131	pur
132	piš, kir, ḳir
133	u
	^{amel}U.MUK
134	lit, liṭ
135	mi
136	kabtu
137	nim
138	eli, muḫ(ḫi)

139	ṣur	159	še
140	karâbu		zêru
141	ul		ŠE.BAR
142	tul		šamaššammu
143	ši, lim; pânu; înu,		išmē, šemē (א, שמע)
	nahrû, mahar; 1000.	160	bu, pu, gid
144	ar	161	ṣir
145	, mudammiķ (דמק)	162	tir, ter
146	û	163	li
147	ru	164	tu
148	pat; kurummatu	165	te
149	man; 20 [= 19]	166	kar, kâru; êṭir (אטר)
150	eš; 30		mušêzib (אזב)
	purussû	167	iddin(a), nâdin, nadin,
151	hum		ittadin (נדן)
152	libittu		šûmu
153	lam	168	kam; êriš (ארש);
154	šêpu		determ. after numerals
155	uk	169	in
156	az, as	170	šar
157	kiš; Kiš	171	ut, tu, par, pir; ûmu
158	mat, lat, šat, nad; šadû		urru
	kurgû	172	Upija

	= 75; = 102	185	me, sip, šib; 100; plural sign.
173	din, tin, dun; bulliṭ, (mu)balliṭ, balâṭu (בלט)	186	meš; plural sign
	Bâbilu	187	lá
174	ḫi; kuzbu	188	ib, ip
175	ʾ(א); sign of a long vowel		v. 32, 81 and cf. 125
176	im; (šâru)	189	upaḫḫir (פחר)
	šûtu	190	lu, dib
	iš/ltânu		immeru
	amurru	191	kin
	šadû		(?) mâr šipri
	šuppu	192	ku; 60; subâtu (det.)
	naʾid (נאד)	193	bul — ašlaku
177	aḫ, iḫ, uḫ	194	sar
178	ḫar, mur	195	šu
	ḫubullu	196	ḫul, ḫal (?)
179	sign of collectivity	197	di, ṭi, ṭe
180	zib sip		dajânu
181	lul	198	ki, ḳi; itti; determ. after names of places
182	esû		šaplû
183	gam		maḫîru
184	gi; išten, šuššu, ana; ⌈1PI;		(?) šuḳultu (šû)
	determ. bef. masc. names	199	1) šaḫ; 2) šul, dun

200 šal, rag; mimmû/a; det. bef. fem. names and prof.

201 dam; aššatu (aššu-)

202 ṣu

203 mimma^ma; v. 200

204 gu

205 amtu

206 nin

207 (with [sign]) nangâru

208 el

209 lib; libbu

210 tar, kut, dim; sûḳu

211 1) šipâtu

2) tuk; iraššî (ירשׁ)

[sign] râšû

212 v. 74

213 kab

v. 28

214 karû

215 ur, lik, liḳ

([sign]) kalbu

216 tu; šiḳlu

217 1/3 (manê) (šuššân)

218 2/3 (šinipu)

219 5/6 (parasrab)

220 2 (šinâ); šanû

221 a; ablu

'a

-šû, -šâ

Akkadû

eḳlu

nâru

ittû

222 ša, nik; GAR (measure) iškun, šâkin (שׁכן)

223 za, ṣa. cf. 228

224 : hurâṣu

šibirtu

kaspu

kudimmu

225 ha

halâḳu

226 4 (irbitti)

227 ya; 5 (hamištu)

To 222 add:

228 kudurru

GLOSSARY. [1]

א **a'** namely, amounting to, *und zwar, nämlich, im Betrage von.* Ideogr. A.AN.

א$_1$א$_2$ל **âlu** town, city, *Stadt.*

אאל **a'âlu** I 1 to bind, to contract (a debt), to draw up (a document), *binden, (eine Schuld) eingehen, (eine Urkunde) ausfertigen*; praet. î'il; perm. i'il, 'il (passive).

u'iltu obligation, record, document, *Verbindlichkeit, Urkunde, Schein*; debt, *Schuld.*

א$_1$ב **abu** father, *Vater*; abu bîti housekeeper, *Hausvater* (a title?), written AD.Ê; probably to be read (following Meissner) AD.KID = addubu, q. v.

Abu (araḫ) the fifth month, *der fünfte Monat.*

אבך **abâku** I 1 to lead, to fetch, to take away, to buy (a slave), *leiten, holen, wegnehmen (einen Sklaven) kaufen*; praet. îbuk, praes. ibbak, perm. abik (passive).

abkallu sage, *Weiser* (?) (PN).

---

1) א$_1$ = arab. أ, א$_2$ = ɤ, א$_3$ = ح, א$_4$ = ع, א$_5$ = غ. ‖ PN = only in proper names. ‖ § = A. Ungnad, *Babylonisch-Assyrische Grammatik* (Munich 1906). ‖ For the difference between ^ and ¯ over a vowel cf. § 3[k].

אבל[1]) **ablu** son, *Sohn.*

abullu f. gate, *Tor.*

ubânu digit, *Zoll* (= $^1/_{24}$ a m m a t u); also a surface measure, *auch Flächenmass.*

אבר₁ **abâru** I 1 to be strong, *stark sein*; inf. a b â r u and abbrev. b â r u strength, *Stärke* (PN).

אבת₁ **abtu** in b î t u a b t u lit. destroyed house, *zerstörtes Haus*; i. e. the place (plot) where a building has been pulled down, *Abbruchgrundstück*; but perhaps better to be read ^{bît}a p t u dwellinghouse, *Wohnhaus.*

אגר₃ **agurru** kiln-baked brick, *Backstein.*

addubu ship-wright, *Schiffbauer* (?); cf. a b u b î t i.

אדי₄ **adī** 1) praep. (§ 56^{b}) until (inclusively), *bis* (*einschliesslich*); a d ī 3ta š a n â t i for three years, *auf drei Jahre*; a d ī 1 2 - t a - a - a n to the twelvefold amount, *bis zum zwölffachen Betrage*; 2) subj. (§ 61), also a d i m u ḫ ḫ i (š a) till, until, *bis* (*dass*).

udê (plur.) furniture, *Hausgerät.*

אדר₁ **Addaru** (a r a ḫ) the twelfth month, *der zwölfte Monat*; ^{araḫ}A d d a r u a r k û the intercalary (13th) month, *Schaltmonat* (= *dreizehnter Monat*).

אדר₂ **adâru** I 1 to fear, to honor, *fürchten*, *ehren*; praet. ê d u r.

אור₁ **urru** (cf. § 3^{d}) light, *Licht* (PN).

---

1) Stem uncertain.

אזב$_4$ **ezêbu** III 1 to save, *retten* (PN).

אח$_1$ **aḫu** brother, *Bruder;* plur. a ḫ ḫ ê (§ 21^{m}) (PN).

aḫameš (§ $57^{a\alpha}$) each other, *einander.*

אטר$_4$ **eṭêru** I 1 a) to spare, to rescue (with i n a) *schonen, retten*; part. ê ṭ e r u (PN); b) to pay, *bezahlen*; inf. e-ṭe-ru, e-ṭer-ru (§ 3^{d}); praet. î ṭ i r; perm. to have been paid, to have received, *bezahlt sein, erhalten haben.*

אין$_1$ **yânu** v. sub י.

אין$_4$ **înu** eye, *Auge* (PN).

איר$_1$ [1] **Ayaru** (a r a ḫ, later pronunciation probably r u) the second month, *der zweite Monat.*

akî for, at the rate of, *für, zum Preise von.*

êkurru temple, *Tempel* (PN).

אל$_1$ **ilu** god, *Gott.*

ul (§ 59^{b}) not, *nicht.*

altu v. אנש$_1$.

אלי$_4$ **ėlû** (§ 53^{e}) I 1 to go up, to be found, to occur, to take place, *hinaufgehen, sich finden, auftauchen, stattfinden*; praes. i l l ī, e l l ī.

elû upper, *oberer.*

elī = m u ḫ ḫ i q. v.

elat, e l a t (t u m) š a (§ 56^{c}) except, besides, *ausser, abgesehen von.*

אלך$_1$ **alâku** (§ 47^{h}) I 1 to go, *gehen*; praes. i l l a k.

אלל$_1$ **Elûlu** (a r a ḫ) the sixth month, *der sechste Monat.*

ellatu strength, *Stärke* (PN).

---

1) Stem perhaps אור$_1$

אלף$_1$ **alpu** bull, *Stier.*

elippu ship, *Schiff.*

ultu 1) praep. (§ 56^b) from, *von . . . an*; 2) subj. (§ 61), also ultu (muḫḫi) ša after, *nachdem.*

אם$_1$ **amtu** female slave, *Sklavin*; amat-šarrûtu (§ 24^m) the state of being the king's (female) slave, *Stellung einer Königssklavin.*

אמד$_4$ **imittu** tax paid in kind, *Naturalienabgabe* (?); perhaps also, harvest, *Ertrag.*

אמי$_3$ **amâtu** word, *Wort* (PN).

U.MUK (amêl) a title (profession ?) of uncertain meaning, *ein Titel (Beruf?) unsicherer Bedeutung.*

אמל **amêlu** man, *Mann, Mensch*; often only determinative.

amêlûtu, amêluttu (§ 3^d) servant(s), *Gesinde, dienende Person.*

אמם$_1$ **ummu** mother, *Mutter.*

ummā (§ 57$^{b\gamma}$) as follows, *folgendermassen.*

ammatu yard, *Elle* (= $^1/_7$ ḳanû), also a surface measure, *auch Flächenmass.*

אמר$_1$ **amâru** I 1 to look, *schauen*; impv. amur. opt. lîmur (PN).

immeru sheep, *Schaf.*

amurru west, *Westen.*

ana (§ 56^b) to, for, at the price of, upon, against, *zu, für, zum Preise von, auf, gegen,* (*umschreibt den Dativ*); with the infin. (§ 32$^{f\gamma}$) in order to, that he (etc.) might, *um . . . zu, auf dass* *er (etc.) . . . möge*; ana muḫḫi to the debit of, *zu jemandes Lasten.*

ina (§ 56^{b}) in, at, among, out . . . of, as, *in, bei, unter, aus, als*; ina muḫḫi to the debit of, to be paid by, against, *zu jemandes Lasten, zu zahlen von, gegen*; ina ḳâti from the hand of, from, *aus jemandes Hand, von.*

ân (a-an) distributive particle, *Distributivpartikel* (= each, *je, jeder*).

אני$_4$ **enû** (§ 53^{e}) I 1 to change, to make alterations, *ändern, Änderungen treffen*; praes. innī.

anâkū (§ 10) I, *ich.*

אנן$_1$ **annû** (§ 12^{b}) this, *dieser*; fem. annîtu.

אנש$_1$ **aššatu** (§ 6^{f}), altu (§ 5$^{c\alpha}$, § 6^{i}) wife, *Ehefrau.*

aššûtu state of being a wife, wifehood, *Stellung einer Ehefrau.*

אסי$_1$ **usâtu** help, *Hilfe* (PN).

aptu f. dwelling-house, *Wohnhaus*; cf. abtu (אבת$_1$).

אפל **apâlu** I 1 to pay, *bezahlen*; perm. passive. I 3 = I 1.

אפר **epru** food, *Speise.*

אפש **epêšu** I 1 to make, *machen*; praet. îpuš (PN).

אקל$_3$ **eḳlu** field, plot, *Feld, Grundstück.*

aḳru v. יקר.

ardu v. ורד.

ûru surrounding, *Umhegung* (?), perhaps in the phrase u-ri i-ša-an-nu (שני?).

urû stable, *Stall*.

ארץ₁ **irṣitu** land, quarter of a town, ward, *Land, Stadtviertel, Bezirk*.

urru v. אור₁.

ארש₆ **erêšu** I 1 to plant, *pflanzen*; praet. êreš (cf. § 5bα); part. êreš; perm. ereš (PN).

mêrišu plantation, *Pflanzung*.

ašgandu (amêl) governor, *Verwalter* (?).

אשי **ešû** I 1 to confound, *verwirren*; infin. ešû perturbance, *Verwirrung* (PN).

ašlakû (amêl) fuller, *Walker* (?).

אשר₁ **ašar** (§ 61aβ) where, *wo, wohin*.

אשר₄ **ešrû** tithe, *Zehnt*.

ašaridu (amêl) chief, officer, *Anführer, Offizier*; also abbreviated (PN) šarid.

aššatu v. אנש₁.

ištu (§ 56b) from, *von . . . her*.

ištânu, iltânu (§ 6i) north, *Norden*.

išten one, *einer*; fem. ištît (cf. rittu); ištena-a-an šaṭâru ilteḳû they received one document each, *sie empfingen je eine Urkunde*.

išteniš (§ 57aα) one like the other, *einer wie der andere*.

את **iti** adjoining, *angrenzend an*.

itti (§ 56b) with, from, *mit, von*.

ittî simultaneously, together, *gleichzeitig, zugleich*.

ittû asphaltum, *Asphalt*.
אתל **etellu** lord, *Herr* (PN).
etellitu lady, *Herrin* (PN).
אתק. **etêḳu** III 1 to let advance, *vorrücken lassen* (PN).

ב.

באל. **bêlu** lord, *Herr*.
bêltu lady, *Herrin* (PN).
באר **bâ'iru** (a m ê l) fisherman, *Fischer*.
I. bâbu child, *Kind* (PN).
II. bâbu a) gate, *Tor*; b) time, *Mal*.
bâbtu outstanding, unpaid money (etc.), *ausstehendes, unbezahltes Geld (etc.)*.
בוש **bâšu** I 1 to be disgraced, *zu Schanden werden* (PN).
II 1 to put to shame, *zu Schanden werden lassen* (PN).
בחר **biḫiru** (a m ê l) a title of uncertain meaning, *ein Titel unsicherer Bedeutung*.
biltu v. ובל.
בין **bânu** I 1 to give, *geben*; impv. b î n.
בית **bîtu** house, *Haus*.
בלט **balâṭu** I 1 to live, *leben*; inf. b a l â ṭ u life, *Leben* (PN).
II 1 to keep alive, *am Leben erhalten* (PN); u-b u l-l i ṭ = u b a l l i ṭ; b u l-ṭ u = b u l l i ṭ.
בני **banû** I 1 to build, to create, *bauen, schaffen*;

praet. ibnī, part. bânī, perm. banī, fem. banât (PN).

bânû (amêl) builder, *Bauhandwerker*; amêl rab bânî architect, *Baumeister*.

mâr-bânûtu v. mâru (מאר₂).

bâru v. אבר₁.

בשי **bašû** I 1 perm. to be, to exist, *sein*, *existieren*.
III 1 to call into existence, *ins Dasein rufen* (PN).
III 2 = III 1.
IV 2 to be called into existence, *ins Dasein treten* (PN).

בתל **batûltu** virgin, *Jungfrau*.

bitlê [1]) a sort of spice, *eine Art Gewürz*.

בתק[2]) **batḳu** care, *Sorge* (?); batḳu ša ... ṣabâtu to take care for (the good condition of), *sich kümmern (um den guten Zustand von etwas)* [3]).

ג.

gabrû duplicate, *Duplikat*.

gugallu (amêl) manager, *Vorsteher*.

גדל **gidlu**, gid-dil string, a measure for onions, *Schnur*, *Mass für Zwiebeln*.

---

1) Reading and derivation quite uncertain.

2) Or בדק, בטק?

3) For this meaning cf. *Cuneiform Texts of the British Museum* XXII, 116 l. 15; *Vorderasiatische Schriftdenkmäler* V 10, l. 7; VI 290 Strassmaier, *Nabuch.* 90, l. 15 (read [*ṣa*]-*bat*).

gûzu element in PN of uncertain meaning, *Element in Eigennamen, Bedeutung unsicher.*

gallu v. ḳallu.

גמל **gamâlu** I 1 to spare, *schonen* (PN).

gimillu present, *Geschenk* (PN).

גמר **gamru** full, *voll;* kasap gamirti the sum total, *die ganze Summe.*

gamrûtu fullness, completeness, *Vollständigkeit;* šîm gamrûti full price, *voller Preis.*

ginû sacrifice, *Opfer;* amêlNI.ŠUR GI.NA (= ginê) superintendent of the sacrifices, (?) *Opferaufseher* (?).

gurru (better to be read kurru) a measure of capacity, also a surface measure, *Flächen- und Hohlmass;* cf. p. 40.

gišimmaru datepalm, *Dattelpalme.*

ד.

Du'ûzu (araḫ) the fourth month, *der vierte Monat.*

דבב **dabâbu** I 1 to speak, *sprechen;* dînu dabâbu to carry on a lawsuit, *prozessieren;* praes. idibbub; inf. dabâbu speech, agreement, *Rede, Abmachung.*

dibbu speech, agreement, matter, *Rede, Abmachung, Angelegenheit.*

דגל **dagâlu** I 1 to look upon, *auf jemanden blicken* (PN).

I 2 (with pâni NN.) to be at the disposal of NN., *dem NN. zur Verfügung stehen.*

III 1 (with pâni NN.) to place at the disposal of NN., *dem NN. zur Verfügung stellen.*

דוך **dâku** I 1 to strike, to kill, *schlagen*, *töten*; perm. dîki (cf. § 50[b]) passive.

דור **dûru** wall, *Mauer.*

דין **dânu** I 1 to judge, *richten* (PN).

dînu lawsuit, *Prozess.*

dayânu (da'ânu, dânu) judge, *Richter.*

dikû (amêl) a title of uncertain meaning, *Titel unsicherer Bedeutung*; fem. dikîtu.

דמק **damâḳu** I 1 to be pure, beautiful, *rein*, *schön sein* (PN).

II 1 to make pure, beautiful, *rein, schön machen* (PN).

damḳu pure, beautiful, *rein, schön* (PN).

dumḳu purity, beauty, *Reinheit, Schönheit* (PN).

דנן **I dannu** strong, *stark* (PN).

II. dannu (karpat) barrel, *Fass.*

ו.

û and, also, *und, auch.*

ובל **abâlu** to carry, to fetch, *bringen*, *holen*; for ublûnimmā cf. § 48[h].

biltu talent, *Talent* (= 60 manê).

וצא **aṣû** I 1 to come forth, *herausgehen*; opt. lûṣī (PN).

mûṣû exit, lane, *Ausgang*, *Gasse.*

ורד **ardu** slave, *Sklave;* arad-šarrûtu (§ 24m) the state of being the king's slave, *Stellung eines Königssklaven.*

ורח **arḫu** month, *Monat.*

(W)araḫsamnu (araḫ) the eighth month, *der achte Monat.*

ורך **arki** (§ 56c) after, after the death of, *nach, nach jemandes Tode.*

arkû later, *späterer;* fem. arkîtu; cf. Addaru.

ושב **ašâbu** (inf.) presence, *Gegenwart, Beisein.*

ותר **atru** surplus, *Überschüssiges.*

ז.

זכי **zakû** I 1 perm. to be free of obligation, *frei von Verpflichtung sein.*

זכר **zakâru** I 1 to call, swear, *rufen, schwören;* praet. izkur.

זקף **zaḳpu** (§ 32fδ) planted, *bepflanzt;* gišimmarê zaḳpu planted with (§ 19g) datepalms, *mit Dattelpalmen bepflanzt.*

זר.א **zêru** seed, progeny, cornfield, *Same, Nachkommenschaft, Kornfeld.*

ח.

חבי[1] **ḫibû** I 1 to break, to cancel, *zerbrechen, ungültig machen;* praes. iḫibbī; perm. ḫibī (passive).

II 1 = I 1.

1) Originally חפי.

ḫibû broken, *zerbrochen.*

חבל **ḫubullu** interest, *Zins.*

חדי **ḫadû** II 1 inf. ḫuddû in ḫud libbi free will, *freier Wille.*

ḫazannu prefect, sheikh, *Ortsvorsteher, Scheich.*

חלק **ḫalâḳu** I 1 to perish, *zugrunde gehen*; inf. ḫal-la-ki ruin, *Untergang.*

I 2 to run away, *fortlaufen.*

halḳu destroyed, lost, *zerstört, verloren gegangen.*

ḫalluru = $^{1}/_{10}$ (?) šiḳlu.

חמש **ḫamištu** five, *fünf.*

ḫummušu divided into five parts, *in fünf Teile geteilt*; also = $^{1}/_{5}$ šiḳlu.

חסס **taḫsitu,** vulg. = taḫsistu notice, reminder, *Notiz, Mahnung* (?).

חפי v. חבי.

ḫuṣêtu hamlet, *Weiler* (?).

חרץ **ḫarîṣu** fixed, *festgesetzt.*

ḫurâṣu gold, *Gold.*

ḫarrânu road, *Strasse.*

חתן **ḫatanu** son-in-law, *Schwiegersohn.*

ט.

Ṭebêtu (araḫ) the tenth month, *der zehnte Monat.*

טוב **ṭâbu** good, *gut* (PN).

ṭabtu [1]) ṣalt, *Salz.*

---

1) Stem quite uncertain.

טחי **ṭaḫu** (tâḫ) adjoining, *angrenzend an.* Ideogr. UŚ.SA.DU[1]).

י.

יד **idu** rent, *Miete.*

ידא **idû** (§ 53g) I 1 to know, *wissen.*

יום **ûmu** 1) day, *Tag*; 2) subj. (§ 61aγ) when, if, *wenn.*

yânu non-existence, *Nichtexistenz*; praedicative: there is not, *es gibt nicht*; ana idi bîti yânu under the condition that no rent is to be paid, *unter der Bedingung, dass keine Miete bezahlt wird.*

יקר **aḳru** dear, *teuer* (PN).

ירב **erêbu** I 1 to increase, *vermehren*; impv. erba.

ישי **išû** (§ 53g) I 1 to have, *haben.*

ישר **ešêru** I 1 to thrive, *gedeihen*; opt. lîšir (PN).

כ.

כבת **kabtu** honored, mighty, *geehrt, mächtig* (PN).

kudimmu goldsmith, *Goldschmied.*

kidinnu client, *Klient* (PN).

kudurru servant, *Diener* (?) (PN).

כום **kûmu** (§ 56c) instead of, for, *anstatt, für.*

כון **kânu** II 1 to establish, to testify, *festsetzen, bezeugen*; part. amêl mukinnu witness, *Zeuge.*
II 2 = II 1.

kînu, ki-in-nu (§ 3d) firm, true, *fest, wahr* (PN).

kittu (§ 18b.h) truth, *Wahrheit.*

---

1) Cf. *Vorderasiatische Schriftdenkmäler* V 64, l. 2; 78, l. 2; 82 l. 2; 121, l. 6. 7.

כזב **kuzbu** abundance, *Überfluss* (PN).

כי **kî** 1) praep. (§ 56b) like, according to, for, *wie, gemäss, für*; 2) subj. (§ 61a) when, if, *wenn*.

kî'am thus, *so*.

kîmā (§ 56b) like, instead of, *wie, anstelle*.

kîtu v. קתי.

kimtu family, *Familie*.

כלב **kalbu** dog, servant, *Hund, Diener* (PN).

kalakku cellar, *Keller* (?).

כלם **kalâmu** II 1 to show, *zeigen*.

כנך **kanâku** I 1 to seal, to draw up (a document), *siegeln, (eine Urkunde) ausfertigen*; praet. ik-nuk; amêlkânik bâbi notary, *Notar* (?).

kunukku seal, *Siegel*.

Kislimu (araḫ) the ninth month, *der neunte Monat*.

כסף **kaspu** silver, money, *Silber, Geld*.

כפר **kupru** bitumen, *Erdharz*.

כצר **kaṣâru** I 1 to preserve, *bewahren* (PN).

kâru rampart, quay (?), *Wall, Quai* (?).

karû storehouse, *Speicher*.

kirû garden, *Garten*.

כרב **karâbu** I 1 to bless, *segnen* (PN).

kiribtu blessing, *Segen* (PN).

kurgû fowl, *Huhn*.

כרי **karû** II 1 to shorten, *verkürzen*.

כרם **kurummatu** food, maintenance, *Speise, Nahrung, Unterhalt*.

karpatu pot, *Topf*; often only determinative, *oft nur Determinativ.*

kurru v. g u r r u.

כשד **kišâdu** neck, bank, *Hals, Ufer.*

כשר **kešêru** I 1 to consolidate, to support, *festigen, unterstützen*; part. k i - š i r, i. e, k ê š e r (PN).

כתר **kitru** alliance, ally, *Bündnis, Bundesgenosse* (PN).

ל.

לא₁ **lâ** (§ 59a) not, *nicht.*

לאי₁ **li'û** mighty, *mächtig* (PN).

לבב **libbu** heart, midst, *Herz, Mitte*; ḫ u d l i b b i v. חדי; i n a l i b b i among (that number), *unter, darunter.*

libbû in ŠAG - u e ḳ l i of uncertain meaning, *Bedeutung unsicher.*

לבן **libittu** (§ 18h) sun-dried brick, *ungebrannter Ziegel.*

לבש **lubûšu,** l u b u š t u (sometimes with the determinative ṣ u b â t) garment, clothes, *Kleid, Kleidung.*

לו **lû** (§ 58e) particle to indicate the optative, *Optativpartikel.*

לקא **liḳû** I 2 to take, *nehmen.*

latanu female servant, *Dienerin* (?).

מ.

-mā (§ 58a) enclitic particle 1) used to strengthen a word, *dient zur Hervorhebung eines*

Wortes; 2) connected with the verb (§ 32e): then, in that case, thereupon, according (to which), *dann, in diesem Falle, darauf, gemäss (dessen u. s. w.)*.

מא₂ר **mâru** son, child, *Sohn, Kind*; m â r š ū š a (§ 24o) son of, *Sohn von*; m â r - b â n û t u (§ 24m) the state of being a free man, *Stellung eines Freien*; t u p p u m â r - b â n û t u document of manumission, *Freilassungsurkunde*; m â r š i p r i messenger, *Bote*.

mârtu daughter, *Tochter* (cf. m â r u); TUR. SAL-A.NI = m â r t u š ū/ā, m â r a t s ū/ā; m â r a t 3ta š a n â t i three years old, *dreijährig*.

mûrânu young lion, *junger Löwe* (PN).

מות **mâtu** I 1 to die, *sterben*; perm. m î t.

מחח **muḫḫi** (§ 56c, = e l ī) upon, on, *auf*; (i n a) m u ḫ ḫ i on the debit of, to be paid by, over, *zu jemandes Lasten, zu zahlen von, über*.

מחר **maḫâru** I 1 to receive, to buy, *empfangen, kaufen*; praet. i m ḫ u r; perm. 1) to have received, bought, *empfangen, gekauft haben*; 2) to please, *belieben*.

I 2 (a n - d a - ḫ a r § 6eα, § 6mα) = I 1 (PN).

maḫar (§ 56c) before, in the presence of, *vor, in Gegenwart von*.

miḫrat (§ 56c) opposite, *gegenüber*.

maḫîru (purchase-)price, *Kaufpreis*.

maḫrû former, *früherer*; fem. m a ḫ r î t u.

malā 1) (§ 16c) whatever, *alles was*; 2) (praep.) according to, *gemäss*.

malaḫu (a m ê l) sailor, *Schiffer*.

מלך **malâku** I 2 to deliberate, *beraten*.

mâliku councellor, *Ratgeber* (PN).

mimmû (§ 15c) all the property belonging to somebody, *alles was jemand besitzt*.

minû (§ 14a) what?, *was?*

מני **manû** I 1 to count, *zählen*.

manû mine, *Mine* (= 60 š i ḳ l u).

mûṣû v. וצא$_1$.

מקת **muḳuttû** (false) claim for damages, (*falscher*) *Schadenanspruch*.

משי **mašû** I 1 to forget, *vergessen*.

משח **mašîḫu** measure, *Mass*; m a š î ḫ u š a s a t t u k a certain measure (especially for cereals), containing a little more than the ordinary m a š î ḫ u, *ein bestimmtes Mass* (*besonders für Naturalien*), *etwas grösser als das gewöhnliche* m a š î ḫ u.

משך **maškânu** pledge, *Pfand*.

mišlu half, *Hälfte*.

משר **mašâru** II 1 to leave, *lassen*; with i n a p â n i: to place at the disposal of, *jemandem zur Verfügung stellen*.

matîma whenever, *wann immer*.

נ.

נאד **na'âdu** I 1 to exalt, *erheben*; perm. passive, erhaben (PN).

נ׳אר **nâru** river, canal, *Strom, Fluss, Kanal.*

נב׳א **nabû** (§ 53[c]) I 1 to call, to agree with, *rufen, vereinbaren*; praet. imbē (§ 6p[α]).

nubtu bee, *Biene* (PN).

נגר **nâgiru** overseer, *Aufseher* (PN).

naggâru, nangâru (§ 6 p[α]) carpenter, *Zimmermann.*

נדד v. נדן.

נדן **nadânu** I 1 to give, to sell, *geben, verkaufen*; praet. iddin, iddid, (46, 7), with suffix iddinsu, idaššū; praes. inamdin (§ 6p[α]); impv. idin, id-din (§ 9[a]); perm. passive. I 2 = I 1.

nudunnû dowry, *Mitgift.*

נור **nûru** light, *Licht* (PN).

נזז **nazâzu** I 1 to stand, to be present, *stehen, gegenwärtig sein.*

III 1 to place, *stellen*; praet. ušziz (§ 46g[δ]).

Nîsannu (araḫ) the first month, *der erste Monat.*

nisûtu relatives, *Verwandtschaft* (?).

nisippu a measure of capacity used for measuring oil, *ein Hohlmass zum Messen von Öl.*

נפח **nappâḫu** blacksmith, *Schmied.*

נפש **ištu** soul, *Seele*; plur. life, *Leben.*

נצר **naṣâru** I 1 to protect, *schützen*; praet. iṣṣur; impv. uṣur (PN).

niš (§ 56c) by the name of, *bei.*

נשא **našû** I 1 to raise, to carry, to fetch, to take, *emporheben, tragen, holen, nehmen*; pût... ina ḳât NN. našû (mostly perm.) to be responsible to NN. for, *dem NN. für etwas verantwortlich sein*; pût šêpi NN... našû to be responsible that NN. does not go away, *verantwortlich sein, dass NN. nicht fortgeht*; for perm. na-a-šu and na-aš-šu cf. § 9a.

NI-ŠUR (amêl) v. ginû.

ס.

סדד **sadâdu** II 1 to honor, *ehren.*

סוק **sûḳu** street, *Strasse.*

siḫû claimant, *Reklamant* (?).

salatu kindred, *Sippe* (?).

סלם **salâmu** I 1 to turn to graciously, *sich gnädig zuwenden*; praet. islim (PN).

suluppu date, *Dattel.*

Sîmânu [1]) (araḫ) the third month, *der dritte Monat.*

ספר **sipiru** (amêl) commissioner, *Geschäftsführer* (?).

sattukku fixed sacrifice, *festbestimmtes Opfer*; cf. mašîhu.

---

1) Stem uncertain, perhaps סום.

פ.

pûtu front, broad-side, *Vorderseite, Breitseite*; pût[1]) . . . našû v. נשא.

piḫâtu district, *Bezirk*.

פחר **paḫâru** II 1 to bring together, to give support, *zusammenbringen, Halt geben* (PN).

napḫaru totality, sum total, *Gesamtheit, Summe*.

paḫḫâru potter, *Töpfer*.

פי **pû** mouth, *Mund* (PN).

פלח **palâḫu** I 1 to respect, *Ehrfurcht erweisen*; praet. iplaḫ.

pânu face, *Antlitz*; ina pâni at the disposal of, *zu jemandes Verfügung*; cf. also דגל I 2, III 1.

פסס **pasâsu** II 1 to destroy, to annihilate, *zerstören, annullieren*.

puṣâ'a (amêl) washer, *Wäscher* (?); fem. puṣâ'ìtu.

פקר **pâḳirânu** (paḳ-ḳir-a-ni etc.) plaintiff, *Kläger*.

pir'u offspring, *Sprössling* (PN).

parzillu iron, *Eisen*.

פרס **parâsu** I 1 to decide, *entscheiden*; with ina muḫḫi to pass sentence against, to fine, *gegen jemand erkennen, mit einer Strafe belegen*.

purussû decision, judgment, *Entscheidung, Urteil*.

פשש **piššatu** ointment, *Salböl*.

---

1) Or bûtu? The word has perhaps nothing to do with pûtu front.

פתן **patânu** I 1 to protect, *beschützen*; praet. iptin (PN).

פתק **pitḳu** divided into eight (?) parts, *in acht* (?) *Teile geteilt*; also = $^1/_8$ (?) šiḳlu.

צ.

צ.אר **ṣêru** plain, country, *Ebene*, *Land*.

צבת **ṣabâtu** I 1 to take, to seize, *nehmen*, *ergreifen*; batḳu ṣabâtu v. batḳu.

ṣubâtu garment, *Kleid*; often only determinative, *oft nur Determinativ*.

צחר **ṣaḫru** little, *klein*; fem. ṣaḫirtu.

צלל **ṣillu** shadow, *Schatten* (PN).

צפר **ṣupru** fingernail, *Fingernagel*.

ק.

קבא **ḳibû** I 1 to order, to say, *befehlen*, *sagen*.

ḳibû order, *Befehl* (PN).

קיש **ḳâšu** I 1 to give as a present, *schenken*; praet. iḳîš (PN).

ḳallu servant, *Diener*; fem. ḳallatu.

קמ₃א **ḳîmu** flower, *Mehl*.

ḳanû rod, *Rute* (= $^1/_2$ GAR); also an areal measure, *auch Flächenmass*; plur. ḳanâti (house-)plot, *Grundstück*.

ḳaḳḳadu capital (without interest), *Kapitalsumme (ohne Zinsen)*.

קרב **ḳirbu** (§ 56c) in the midst of, in, *inmitten, in.*

ḳirubû arable, but not yet cultivated ground, *kultivierbares, noch nicht bearbeitetes Land.*

ḳâtu hand, *Hand*; ina ḳâti from, *von*; ša ḳâti entrusted to, *jemandem anvertraut.*

קתי **ḳîtu** end, *Ende.*

ר.

ר׳אי **rê'û** shepherd, *Hirt.*

ר׳אם **râmu** I 1 to love, to be merciful, *lieben, gnädig sein* (PN).

rêmûtu mercy; gift (of mercy), *Gnade, Gnadengeschenk* (PN).

ר׳אש **rêšu** beginning, *Anfang.*

רבי **rabû** I 1 to grow, to increase, to be added, *wachsen, anwachsen, hinzukommen.*

rabû great, eldest, *gross, ältester*; in titles often = chief-, *Ober-*; rab-bîti major-domo, *Majordomus*; rab-šušši commander of sixty soldiers, *Befehlshaber von sechzig Soldaten.*

רגם **ragâmu** I 1 to complain, *Klage führen.*

rugummû complaint, *Klage.*

rîḫu, rîḫtu rest, remainder, *Rest.*

ריק **rêḳu** empty, *leer.*

רכס **rakâsu** I 1 to bind, *binden*; riksu rakâsu

to make a treaty, to contract, *einen Kontrakt machen.*

riksu v. rakâsu.

רפש **rapšu** broad, *breit.*

רשי **rašû** I 1 to take, to get, *nehmen, bekommen* (PN). I 2 = I 1; for ištaššû = irtaššû cf. § 6[h].

râšû (amêl) creditor, *Gläubiger.*

râšûtu credit in favor of somebody, *Guthaben.*

rittu hand, *Hand*; ina ištîtit ritti[1]) all at once, *alles auf einmal.*

ש.

ša 1) (§ 13[a]) the one of, belonging to, claim of, *der von, jemandem gehörig, Forderung von,* ša elī ali city-prefect, *Stadtpräfekt*; ša NN. šinā they belong to NN., *sie gehören dem NN.*; particle of the genitive, *Genetivpartikel* (§ 24[n]); ša arḫi monthly, *monatlich*; 2) used like a preposition: ša mišil kurri for half a kur, *für ein halbes Kur*; 3) relat. (§ 16[b]) (he) who, whoever, (*der*) *welcher, wer immer.*

še'u grain, *Getreide.*

šu'âti (§ 12), šumâti (§ 6[eβ]) this, *dieser.*

ש.אלב **šêlibu** fox, *Fuchs* (PN).

---

1) For this reading cf. especially Nerigl. (ed. EVETTS; v. Introd. p. VIII, note 3) No. 31, l. 6: ina ištîtit(sic!) ri-it-tum.

שבט **Sabâṭu** (a r a ḫ) the eleventh month, *der elfte Monat.*

SE.BAR (f.) barley, *Gerste.*

שבר **šibirtu** price, *Preis.*

שנ.א **šigû** lament, *Wehklage* (PN).

šangû [1]) (= š a g g û, § 6pα) priest, *Priester.*

שדד **šiddu** the longside, *Langseite.*

שדי **šadû** 1) mountain, *Berg* (PN); 2) east, *Osten.*

שום [2]) **šûmu** onion, *Zwiebel.*

šûtu south, *Süden.*

שטר **šaṭâru** document, *Urkunde.*

שי.א **šî** she, *sie* (§ 10).

שים **šâmu** I 1 to buy, *kaufen*; praet. i š â m.

šîmu price, payment, *Preis, Bezahlung.*

šînipu $^2/_3$.

שכן **šakânu** I 1 to put, to place, to establish, *setzen, einsetzen*; praet. i š k u n; perm. passive.

maškânu v. משך.

שלט **šalâṭu** I 1 to have power, *Macht haben.*

שלם **šalâmu** I 1 to be safe, *sicher sein*; also perm. (PN); k a s p u š ū i š a l l i m he is safe with regard to his money, i. e. he has received back his money, *er ist sicher in betreff seines Geldes, d. i. er hat sein Geld zurückerhalten.*

II 1 to keep safe, to compensate, *heil erhalten, ersetzen.*

---

1) Stem uncertain, perhaps שנ.א.
2) Stem uncertain.

šulmânu present, *Geschenk* (PN).

שלש **šullultu** third part, *Drittel*; šullulti or šullul (scribal error?) išten šiḳli = $^1/_3$ šiḳlu.

שם **šumu** name, posterity, *Name, Nachkommenschaft*; for šunšū cf § $6^{e\alpha}$.

šumâti v. šu'âti.

שמ.א **šemû** I 1 to hear, to grant somebody's request, *hören, jemandes Bitte erhören;* praes. išemmē; praet. išmē.

שמן **šamnu** oil, *Öl.*

šamaššammu sesame, *Sesam.*

שן **šattu** (§ 18^h) year, *Jahr*; plur. šanâti.

šinā (§ 10) they, *sie* (fem.).

šangû v. שג.א.

שני **šanû** I 1 to change, *ändern*; also in u-ri i-ša-an-nu?

šanû second, other, *zweiter, anderer*; often with mā: šanammā; fem. šanîtu.

שפי **šipâtu** wool, *Wolle.*

שפך **šapâku** I 1 to pour out, *ausgiessen* (PN).

שפל **šaplû** lower, *unterer.*

šaplânu (§ 56^c) below, *unterhalb.*

שפר **šapâru** I 1 to send, to write, *senden, schreiben*; praet. išpur.

šipru message, *Botschaft*; amêl (or mâr) šipri messenger, *Bote.*

našpartu order (sent by letter), (*schriftlicher*) *Auftrag.*

שקל **šiḳlu** shekel, *Sekel.*

šuḳultu weight, value, *Gewicht, Wert.* Ideogr. KI.LAL; KI.LAL-BI = šuḳultašū.

šaridu = ašaridu q. v.

שרי **Tašrîtu** (araḫ) the seventh month, *der siebente Monat.*

שרר **šarru** king, *König.*

šarrûtu reign, *Regierung.*

šuššu sixty, *sechzig*; cf. rabû.

šuššân $^1/_3$.

šutummu (bît) storehouse, *Speicher.*

šattu v. שן.

ת.

תור **târu** I 1 to come back, to repeat doing something, *zurückkommen, etwas wiedertun.*

II 1 to give back, *zurückgeben.*

taḫsitu v. חסס.

תכל **takâlu** I 1 to trust, *vertrauen*; praet. atkal (PN).

tilû female breast, *weibliche Brust.*

-ta-a-an a distributive ending, *Distributivendung;* cf. adī.

תפף **tuppu** tablet, document, *Tafel, Urkunde.*

tupšarru scribe, *Schreiber.*

www.ingramcontent.com/pod-product-compliance
Lightning Source LLC
Chambersburg PA
CBHW062022040426
42447CB00010B/2107